Thrill: The High Sensation Seeking
Highly Sensitive Person

Tracy M. Cooper, Ph.D.

Invictus Publishing, llc

Thrill: The High Sensation Seeking Highly Sensitive Person

All rights reserved.

Copyright © 2016 by Tracy Cooper

ISBN-13 978-1537444581

Invictus Publishing, llc
2303 South 16th Street
Ozark, MO 65721

Author's website: www.drtracycooper.com

This book is protected under the copyright laws of the United States of America. Any reproduction or other unauthorized use of the author's material herein is prohibited without the express written permission of the author.

Printed by CreateSpace, Charleston, SC
Printed in the United States of America
Published by Invictus Publishing, llc
First printing: September 2016

Table of Contents

ACKNOWLEDGEMENTS

DEDICATION

PREFACE

CHAPTER 1 - PERSONALITY TRAITS - A PRIMER 1

CHAPTER 2 - BEGINNING AT THE BEGINNING - CHILDHOOD 26

CHAPTER 3 - CAREER 53

CHAPTER 4 - RELATIONSHIPS 87

CHAPTER 5 - SELF-CARE 108

CHAPTER 6 - RISKY BEHAVIORS AND THE SENSITIVE SENSATION SEEKER 128

CHAPTER 7 - THE CREATIVE FORCE WITHIN 140

CHAPTER 8 - LIVING IN COMMUNITY 159

CHAPTER 9 - THE TALKING STICK 186

CONCLUSION 222

ABOUT THE AUTHOR 227

Acknowledgements

This book would not have been possible without the dedicated work of numerous researchers over the past nearly six decades. Specifically, I would like to acknowledge and express my appreciation for the work of Marvin Zuckerman and Elaine Aron. Zuckerman conceptualized the trait of sensation seeking and studiously followed its development through many phases including the development of reliable instruments to measure sensation seeking in the populace. Personally, I am extremely grateful for Zuckerman's work because it has helped inform my journey as a sensation seeker and explain some of the behaviors of others in my life. Clarity is invaluable!

The work of Elaine Aron has been personally validating, healing, and inspiring as I sought answers to my own highly sensitive temperament. In time, I realized that much work remains to be carried out to help others in their journeys. This work is part of that careful process and would not have been possible without the steadfast and dedicated research of Dr. Aron and her team of researchers. The work she did has laid a solid, scientific foundation on which broad-based researchers (like myself) are now able to build resources that are accessible to everyone. It is my hope that this work continues to lay the foundation on which future work may be carried out in the interest of providing sound guidance to the many sensitive sensation seekers in the world.

Dedication

Writing a book that is the first of its kind is always a challenge and would not have been possible without the belief and support of many people in my life. From my wife, Lisa, who always believed a book such as this was necessary in the world and encouraged me to "just keep going" to my colleague and friend, Misha Mercer, who set such a stellar example of conscientiousness as to motivate me to, in fact, "just keep going" I now offer this book as proof that what seem like enormous goals are attainable. Eventually, even the highest goals become achievable if we trust in the process of creation and hard work.

The same felt instinct that a book such as this needs to be brought into being ultimately giving voice to the many sensitive sensation seekers of the world, and I dedicate this book to my fellow lovers of the new and novel, the subtle and soft, and the profound and compassionate. Our paths will never be easy or clear, but having our collective voices embodied in this book is healing and validating to so many and will serve as a guidepost for others as they make their way in life.

I also dedicate and acknowledge the love and support of my mother, Georgia (Lucy) and my late father, Claude (Shoat) Cooper, who never lived long enough to see what his studious, artistic, comic-book-reading, KISS fan son would achieve in life. And to my oldest brother, Claude (Junior), I dedicate this work as a healing instrument for our family as we work to bridge the many years and miles.

Lastly, I dedicate this work to my beautiful children: Peter, Allyson, Indianna, Ben, and my step-children: Christopher, Micheal, and Caitlin. Dream big, work hard, and "just keep going!" You'll get there!

Preface

The origins of this book date back several years ago when I was working on the book Thrive: The Highly Sensitive Person and Career. During the interviews I conducted for that book I noticed some of the people (all of whom were highly sensitive people) seemed to be describing the characteristics of high sensation seekers. I identify as a high sensation seeking highly sensitive person myself so was quite intrigued and wished to pursue more study in that area, but stayed the course and completed the study for Thrive and later the book itself. I made a promise to myself however that my next book would delve deeply into the high sensation seeking highly sensitive person. This book is the result of that pledge.

To begin with, I read all of the available research literature on sensation seeking, a personality trait that has been continually studied since the 1960s; then I designed a qualitative research study to learn the lived experiences across a wide range from people who identify as high sensation seeking and highly sensitive. My intent was for the study to touch on the most important aspects of life: childhood, career, relationships, self-care, and the social context within which these factors are situated since this was the first book of its kind. Over the course of many months, I interviewed 35 people (the saturation point I eventually reached) after first asking them to take a shortened version of the Highly Sensitive Person Scale and the Sensation Seeking Self-Test. The mean score (or average) was 38 on the Highly Sensitive Person Scale, out of a possible 42 at the extreme end of the scale. The mode (number listed most frequently) was 7 (with possible answers ranging from one to seven). This result seemed to place the participants in the upper 25% of the scale.

The average score for the Sensation Seeking Self-Test was 15 (out of a possible 20 true for me or not true for me responses). The mode (the number repeated most often) was 17. This scale differentiates male from female cutoffs for being considered high sensation seeking. Eleven represents the cutoff for women and 13 for males. The average score was the same for males and females (the results might be different with a larger sample).

The results of the interviews were then analyzed with particular themes emerging. Based on those themes I carefully constructed this book to reflect as accurately as possible the actual words of each person. Each chapter covers a broad swath of life with rich quotes from the people in the study. This richness is further enhanced by the inclusion of additional research references you are free to read if some point should catch your interest. I have taken care to write the book in such a way as to be as educational as inspirational. While this book is not intended to be a self-help book, it is very likely you will benefit from the time you spend with it. Think of it as a gathering of voices each with their story to tell that will awaken you to the reality of life as experienced by highly sensitive high sensation seekers.

There is a temptation that is very strong in humans to bond tightly together in groups quickly casting anyone who is "different" as the "other." While I present this research with the intent of illuminating the challenges, opportunities, and very real stories of highly sensitive high sensation seekers I refrain from homogenizing us as a group. To assume that we are all alike and should fit a mold is to cast ourselves into the same sort of mold that society is already so very good at and is so dreadful for us.

Rather, my intent is to present the broad cross-section of lived experiences as lived and told by real people, all very different from each other.

Likewise, I avoid casting highly sensitive high sensation seekers as being so very different from highly sensitive people. We are highly sensitive people with a little different twist, but still experience the gift/pain of empathy, become overstimulated at times and need to withdraw and recharge in quiet, notice subtleties in many areas of life, and experience deep, rich inner lives propelled by strong emotions.

Lastly, there is great value in immersing ourselves in the pursuit of greater self-awareness for a time. But, at some point, it is advisable that we go back to our lives with renewed vigor and understanding. To remain too deeply embedded in the experiences of others and research explaining various traits is to run the risk of allowing our thinking (and possibly our actions) to become homogenized. Instead, we should glean every morsel we can over a period of time then return to our lives, which necessarily includes those without the traits since we are a minority in the overall population. In doing so, we provide ourselves with room to grow and blossom into the fullest realizations of ourselves without undue external influence regarding limits, types, or traits. For all of the articulation of traits you will read in this book please remember any and all of these represent a broad spectrum of *possible* behaviors. Your experience may vary.

Notes on the book

Throughout this book, you will see me use the words "sensitive sensation seeker," by which I am referring to the high sensation seeker and the highly sensitive person. I shorten the phraseology only for brevity's sake and readability.

Part 1

As we begin this journey one of the most significant issues I have noted in the various books, papers, and websites devoted to writings about highly sensitive people is a focus on the trait in a present only orientation as if the trait is new and exists only within a current paradigm. Partly this is a failing of approaching the study of personality traits from a western perspective, which seeks to reduce, isolate, and analyze each component by itself trusting that the connections will become apparent in time. Too often what occurs is the opposite, and we encounter fragmented pseudo-knowledge purporting to offer quick fixes and authoritative viewpoints that are often not anchored in any meaningful evidence or overall context.

This was bound to happen, to some degree, as awareness of sensory processing sensitivity increased, but nonetheless is counterproductive in the sense of leading us off into opinion-based directions and viewpoints. In this chapter, I present an overview of personality traits (a short primer if you will) and situate that study within a context based on the best evidence we have at the moment. Let's keep in mind that scientific evidence is ever-evolving as we continue to gather new data and make interpretations. Old theories encounter revisions, while new theories find traction. Likewise, fresh minds and viewpoints explore connectivity between bodies of knowledge establishing what may be intuitive links at first that then become grounded in evidence as researchers continue to work.

As a researcher, I offer you a broader view of sensory processing sensitivity and sensation seeking that most sensitive sensation seekers will likely feel right at home with as we tend to be broad and deep-minded people by nature. I suggest to readers that they spend some time in reflection on each section in the chapter and explore on their own the areas that interest them most. This book, at best, is a broad introduction to sensitive sensation seekers covering quite a wide range of lived experiences across the spectrum of life.

Let's begin this journey with open minds, inquisitive natures, and a sense of discovery in finding out what makes us tick.

Chapter 1
Personality Traits – A Primer

"I am not bound to succeed, but I am bound to live up to what light I have." –Abraham Lincoln

Trait Theory (dispositional theory)

Before we begin to discuss the two personality traits that are the primary focus of this book we should, first, lay the groundwork for how we have arrived at this point where personality traits are considered a viable way to explain human behaviors. Let's begin with a quick overview of some of the underlying philosophical underpinnings that psychologists hold in developing any theory explaining personality.

1. Behavior is thought of as unconscious, biological, or environmental by various theorists. In this sense, behavior is either freely chosen or predetermined.
2. Behavior is determined by one's genetics or by the environment. Most theorists today believe behavior to stem from a combination of both.
3. Human behavior is unique and individual or homogenous and universal.
4. We act out of our initiative or because of external stimuli (behaviorism). Most theorists today believe we act out of both with current circumstances dictating the degree to which we act or react.
5. We are capable of intentionally changing our behaviors through learning and growth opportunities (optimistically), or we are not integral to such a scenario (pessimistic).[1]

Thrill

The question we must ask ourselves is, are we capable of free conscious choice or are we living in an illusion where we think we are consciously choosing our behaviors, yet we are far more influenced by internal and external forces than we are aware of? Most of us would probably prefer to think that we own all of our behaviors and beliefs, but in reality, we are each deeply influenced and guided by certain genetic and environmental factors that contribute to our overall makeup.

If we see a large group of people at first, we will not notice any marked differences between individuals. It's only when we narrow our focus and look at particular people that we begin to see distinct differences. Inevitably factors like social class, gender, and race will become obvious ways of delineating people from each other. Beyond those superficial factors we would have to look much closer, and spend much more time with each individual, to understand how each person acts, thinks, and feels differently from each other. We call those patterns that distinguish one person from another, and that persists over time and situations *personalities*.[2] Within each personality is a constellation of personality traits that make up the overall personality.

Historical overview

If we think of personality traits as adjectives, it is easier to imagine how anyone might apply to a person. Thus, we may say "she is outgoing," "he is hard working," or "they are quiet." What we are observing are descriptors of apparent behavior as we can observe them from the outside. Of course, it is not possible to truly know the contents of any person's mind at a given moment or what they might do in differing circumstances, but if we are aware of some descriptors or traits, we have a better view of that individual overall and his propensities.

How did traits develop?

To uncover how personality traits developed let's first talk about *human nature.* Human nature is the qualities that define us as a unique species. Human nature deals with the common characteristics of humans – the shared motives, goals, and psychological mechanisms that are either universal or nearly universal.[2] *Human nature includes species-typical ways in which we make decisions, respond to environmental stimuli, and the ways we influence and manipulate the world around us.*[2] Personality theory attempts to identify the most important ways in which we differ from among the infinite dimensions of possible differences in a non-arbitrary, evidence-based way.

Traits developed as part of a process that is regarded as capable of producing complex functional design, or *natural selection.*[2] Natural selection produced two broad classes of evolved variants: those playing a role in *survival* and those related to *reproductive* competition. Those variants that interfered with successful adaptation were filtered out, while those that were tributary to the successful solution to an adaptive problem passed through the selection sieve and remained. The filtering process of many generations, interacting with the social, physical, and internal environment, produced characteristics that promoted the reproduction of those who possessed the variants. These may be termed as *adaptations.*[2]

Adaptations

Adaptations require genes to be passed from parent to offspring. In all normal environments adaptations develop reliably among most or all members, though may be expressed differently in a given circumstance. These

Thrill

adaptations, though useful in our ancestor's environments, are not forward-looking or intentional.[2] Rather, the individuals who could, say, detect subtle movements or were highly inquisitive enjoyed a greater advantage (even a slight one) in the environment and were more successful reproductively, while those who could not fail to pass on their genetics.

Adaptations are *evolved psychological mechanisms* manifesting as a set of processes that exist as they do because they solved a specific problem of survival or reproduction recurrently over evolutionary history.[2] The interesting thing about any one adaptation is it may only be evolved to take in a narrow slice of information; raise awareness and understanding of the particular adaptive problem it is facing, and utilize decision rules (If-then statements) to produce an output choice.[2] All of this occurs out of consciousness. If-then statements represent a flurry of mental activity, possibly providing information to other adaptations or manifested behaviors, such as arousal as an output or reflection as an additional input.[2]

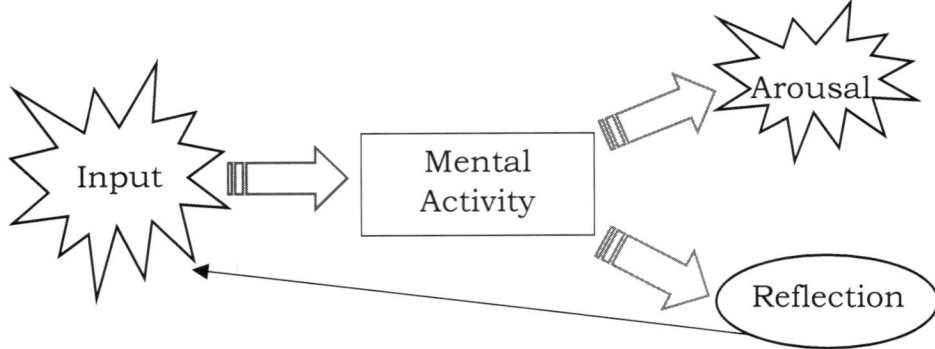

Though these adaptations may or may not lead to a successful solution now they did, on average, lead to successful solutions for our ancestors. You might say why? The likely answer is because all problems are specific and require specificity over generality for several reasons: successful solutions differ from problem to problem; general solutions fail to guide the organism to the correct adaptive solution, and general solutions lead to too many errors which are costly to organisms regarding energy and efforts.[3] Though the idea of limited energy and measured effort seems foreign in modern times when we have ready access to plentiful, nutritious food and clean water in ancestral times, it was a daily struggle to acquire these items. Specific solutions led to specific, efficient answers requiring less spent energy and effort.[2]

As a species we humans possess many evolved psychological mechanisms providing us with behavioral flexibility when encountering survival and reproductive challenges. *The greater our range of possible behaviors the greater our ability to perform well in context-specific ways.* Personality traits, then, represent specific adaptations evolved to meet the challenges of life our ancient ancestors faced on a daily basis for survival and reproduction and may still be present simply because nothing better has come along to replace them.[8]

Has our world really changed?

It may be tempting to think that personality traits worked well in an ancestral age, but times have changed, and our world is entirely different, and certain traits serve no purpose. Or do they? Evolutionary psychologists tell a different story where we may have largely created environments that mimic our Paleolithic limitations and predilections. Cultures may move away from ancestral forms, but the existence of innate biases for certain types of human behavior creates pressures to return to ancestral ways of behaving. They call this tendency *ancestralization*.[2]

In that sense, our arbitrarily created cultures, which form the basis for our material and non-material worlds of belief, tend to liberalize from time to time allowing members of the society to move away from a constrained way of believing and thinking to an ancestral baseline of behavior. For instance, powerful religious, political, and industrial organizations may impose unnatural behaviors or social organizations on society. When those forces begin to lose power people tend to return to a different baseline of behavior that may not reflect the currently existing paradigm. Even now we are witness to enormous forces of liberalization all over our world with deep implications for long-standing power structures. *Many of the problems of human life are simply particular extensions of the problems of primate social life, if on a grander scale.*[2]

Wide reaction norm

As described earlier traits allow for a broad range of possible behaviors across a wide range of potential conditions. Much as the human digestive system is omnivorous, or tolerant of a wide variety of foodstuffs, our personality traits enable us to express problem-specific behaviors geared toward solving either survival or reproductive problems. However, if we find ourselves in conditions that are outside of the range in which the trait developed we may experience physical stress or malfunction. Thus, it is possible that certain traits may exist in ranges that are outside the parameters in which they evolved.

No organism is perfectly adapted to all of the problems in its environment, nor can all organisms possess every trait. However, it is possible for enough individuals to possess a given trait to yield an evolutionary advantage for the community. Similarly, a trait may be relatively dormant in a given culture that proscribes particular behaviors, while discouraging others. *Traits represent possible behaviors, not absolutes.* As we discussed, when a power structure begins to wane in influence and control the tendency of humans is to return to a baseline of behaviors evolved in ancestral times.

How many traits?

Interestingly, there is no consensus regarding exactly how many traits exist. The number ranges from more than 4,000 traits with Gordon Allport, who grouped traits into cardinal, central, and secondary traits with cardinal traits representing traits so dominant in an individual's life they are expressed pervasively; central traits, better thought of as core traits that form the building blocks of personality; and secondary traits, which only occasionally surface.[4]

Psychologist Raymond Cattell narrowed Allport's list to just 16, which he thought of as source traits underlying all personality with each of us expressing any one trait along a spectrum.[5] Thus, we could be low, high, or somewhere in between on any trait. Building on this conceptualization psychologist Hans Eysenck suggested there were just three traits: introversion/extraversion, emotional stability/emotional instability, and, later, psychoticism, which encompassed an individual's capacity for psychotic or sociopathic tendencies.[6]

These theories, and let's remember that a theory is the best conceptualization available at any given moment, gave way to Costa and McRae's popular Five Factor Theory, which distils personality into five broad dimensions: openness, conscientiousness, extraversion, agreeableness, and neuroticism.[7] The OCEAN acronym sometimes is easier to remember. The Five Factor Theory is the most widely accepted theory at this time. You may have noticed that sensory processing sensitivity (SPS hereafter) is nowhere to be found in the Five Factor Theory? SPS is either grouped with neuroticism or ignored altogether, which is interesting because highly sensitive people can be described by any of the five factors, but especially conscientiousness and openness, which sensitive sensation seekers are typically high in.

No consensus

With all of the impressive research that has been conducted into developing a complete conceptualization of personality through trait theory, there still is no consensus about the number of traits or how reliable they might be in a given circumstance. Some criticize trait theory for that very reason; others point to deficiencies in understanding how or why traits emerge in different individuals. With this knowledge can we presume that trait theory is valid and reliable? In my view, yes, we can proceed knowing that we have the best understanding available in our time while acknowledging its inherent shortcomings. There is still much to be gleaned from an intensive study of personality traits in helping us gain greater self-awareness, coming to an acceptance of who we seem to be, and adapting our lives to align better with our unique and individualized needs, values, and aims.

Other theories

Are there other theories that attempt to explain personality? Yes, there are four major perspectives, inclusive of the trait perspective.

- The *psychoanalytic* perspective – emphasizing the importance of early childhood and the unconscious mind, e.g. Freud, Jung, Adler, Erikson, and Horney.

- The *humanistic* perspective – emphasizing psychological growth, free will, and personal awareness, e.g. Rogers, Maslow, and Dabrowski.
- The *trait* perspective – focusing on identifying and measuring unique traits in each individual to better understand personality, e.g. Eysenck, Cattell, McRae, and Costa.
- The *social cognitive* perspective – focusing on social, observational learning, situational influences, and the cognitive processes, e.g. Bandura.

Each of these theories has a storied history with familiar names most of us would recognize, but few would grasp the importance of because, for the most part, psychology has focused on the pathologies of human suffering and how to alleviate them. More recently, of course, there has been positive psychology, which examines how we function at our best, e.g. Seligman and Csikszentmihalyi. Trait theory, then, is one perspective attempting to explain the differences between people through identifying more or less stable patterns of predictable behavior.

If we each possess numerous personality traits, doesn't it get quite complicated in determining how any one trait may be underlying any one behavior? Also, how do they interact and how does that interaction determine behavior? These questions are extremely valid, and we will attempt to pull these definitions apart and unpack a better understanding of each as we focus our attention on just two traits: sensation seeking and sensory processing sensitivity.

Sensation seeking

Thrill

The personality trait known as sensation seeking was established primarily through the work of researcher and psychologist Marvin Zuckerman who has published numerous articles in respected, peer-reviewed journals and published several books on the subject. Sensation seeking, as an evolutionary adaptation aimed at aiding our species in problems of survival and reproduction, can be thought of as a greater willingness (and openness) to approach new stimuli and new situations. The advantage is greater access to potential food sources and mates. A *moderately high* level of the trait expressed in a sufficient number of individuals likely provided an advantage and counterpoint to those on the low end of sensation seeking who preferred to remain in a given area, even if resources ran low.

Zuckerman's Sensation-Seeking Scale, a self-test, has been reinterpreted several times emphasizing one aspect over another and applied in unique ways including attempts to mitigate risky behavior in teens and adults. His work established sensation seeking as a trait not given enough importance in "influencing many diverse kinds of human behavior."[8] The current conceptualization of sensation seeking is a "trait defined by the seeking of varied, novel, complex, and intense sensations and experiences, and the willingness to take physical, social, legal, and financial risks for the sake of such experience."[7] Let's look at the four aspects that make up the sensation seeking construct.

Thrill and adventure seeking

Many people quickly seize on the risk-taking aspect associated with one factor in sensation seeking (thrill and adventure seeking) as not like them, but Zuckerman described risk-taking as a "correlate not an essential part of the definition."[7] His reasoning is based on the idea that sensation seekers accept or underestimate the risk in order to achieve the experience of the sensation. Once we understand this reasoning (and envision sensation seeking as more than simply risk-taking) sensation seeking becomes accessible as a broader construct.

In my study of sensitive sensation seekers roughly 20% described themselves as risk takers aligning themselves with thrill and adventure seeking. This segment of the population prefers taking physical risks that provide a "kick" or thrill like skydiving, snowboarding, downhill skiing, bungee jumping, driving fast in cars and many other examples.

Experience or novelty seeking.
Here the individual seeks out new or novel experiences simply for the sake of the experience itself. These experiences may or may not entail some risk on the part of the individual. This need may be driven by strong curiosity and openness to new experiences. Additionally, sensation seeking has been shown to be strongly correlated to divergent thinking (creativity). Experience and novelty seekers enjoy their thrills through the new experiences they seek out in in unfamiliar places, meeting unfamiliar people, and doing unfamiliar things.

Disinhibition.
This aspect of sensation seeking involves a willingness to step outside societal parameters in search of sensation. Individuals may participate in parties, have

varied sexual partners or experiences, take drugs to facilitate altered states of consciousness, create euphoric moods, increase energy, and decrease boredom. Risk-taking may obviously be involved in this and in a way that was not apparent in our first discussion of risk-taking (as thrill seeking). Risk-taking and disinhibition may involve a calculated or miscalculated appraisal of the risk leading to legal, financial, personal, or emotional consequences. As part of the approach/avoid paradigm disinhibition may serve as an activating mechanism (boldness) that propels an individual forward to investigate regardless of the actual risk.

Boredom susceptibility.

Inner states where the person feels like they are not stimulated within a personally defined range of optimal arousal may experience boredom. Boredom is an aversive state as well as an emotional one where one's mood is markedly down. For many sensation seekers boredom is a "worst enemy," and one they will go to great lengths to avoid. A propensity for boredom can have far-reaching effects in a person's life on social, career, and relationship levels.

The construct

Combined thrill and adventure seeking, experience or novelty seeking, disinhibition, and boredom susceptibility forms a constellation of traits we refer to as sensation seeking. The trait is largely heritable, some 58%, which is significantly higher than the 30-50% range for all other traits.[7] Heritability is further backed up by studies of twins.[9] Sensation seeking is moderated by interactions with the environment influencing how the trait is expressed. The dopamine uptake receptor gene is known as DRD4 (and possibly other as yet unidentified gene/s) seems to be responsible for the genetic expression of the novelty seeking and impulsivity aspects of the trait.[10] The DRD4 gene is sometimes called the "Wanderlust" gene and may be responsible for migrations of humans around the globe. I suggest we call it the "Star Trek" gene considering that sensation seekers are more than willing to "boldly go where no one has gone before."

Sensation seeking is positively related to the presence of gonadal hormones, specifically testosterone in males. High levels of testosterone in males also seem to make them higher on the disinhibition and thrill and adventure seeking subscales.[7] The role of monoamine oxidase (MAO) has also been explored for its possible contributions to sensation seeking at lower levels. Sensation seekers tend to have lower levels of MAO. Low levels of MAO are associated with alcohol, tobacco, marijuana and other forms of substance use and abuse.[11] Sensation seeking tends to peak early in life then taper off as we age, except for the boredom susceptibility, which remains fairly constant throughout life.

Sensory processing sensitivity

Based on the research of Aron and Aron[12] and Aron, Aron and Jagiellowicz[13] sensory processing sensitivity is a personality trait present in 15-20 percent of the worldwide population. Highly sensitive people (those who have SPS as a trait) process experience more deeply — fueled by emotion — with no difference in the sense organs themselves. Highly sensitive people subjectively process experience before acting, may be overstimulated by certain highly individualized sensory input, are aware of subtleties before others, and are highly creative, intuitive, empathic, and conscientious.[14] Seventy percent of HSPs are introverted, while 30 percent are extraverted; approximately one-third to one-half (possibly more) of HSPs experienced unhappy childhoods predisposing them to depression, anxiety, and other psychological issues; approximately one half of HSPs experienced happy childhoods and may be no different than others except in terms of their sensitivity; lastly, HSPs tend to be more deeply affected by positive and negative experiences than others due to the depth of cognitive and emotional processing.[9] Jaeger, described HSPs as intense, which seems to be an apt descriptor given the above definitions.[15]

Sensory processing sensitivity (SPS) is an innate personality trait that is often confused with introversion and shyness. Introversion, while also a trait, is primarily a measure of sociability; shyness is a learned behavior based on past negative social experiences.[9] Taken as a whole we see a group of individuals who think and feel deeply, with a trait that is not widely understood (though this is changing) or accepted as normative.[11] Introverted HSPs, due to their quiet demeanors and propensity for thinking before acting may appear to others as complex, aloof, unfriendly, and even unintelligent.[16] Extraverted HSPs may appear similar to other extraverts, yet may be overwhelmed by too much stimulation and need to withdraw and recharge. This need may lead others to believe they are neurotic or fragile in spite of their sociability.[11]

SPS, like sensation seeking, is likely heritable. Researchers at the University of Copenhagen propose that SPS "may describe an underlying characteristic more directly associated with the 5-HTTLPR genotype. SPS is associated with the enhanced neural processing of detailed visual stimuli and increased neural activation in response to happy and sad faces. This research has also proposed that several of the defining characteristics of SPS are similar to physiological characteristics found in 5-HTTLPR short allele carriers, including increased brain activation in response to emotional stimuli, increased startle response, and increased cortical response to social evaluation. These researchers believe that high levels of SPS may reflect an endophenotype associated with the serotonin transporter 5-HTTLPR short/short genotype."[17]

The conclusion of the Copenhagen study indicates that SPS "describes a psychological profile associated with the homozygotic status of a common polymorphism in the serotonin system."[14] Another study, conducted at Beijing Normal University, found that polymorphisms in TH, DBH, SLC6A3, DRD2, NLN, NTSR1, and NTSR2 were associated with SPS.[18] As with many traits, it is likely there is more than one gene influencing how the various aspects of each trait are expressed. SPS is a complex construct that confounds many people, even HSPs, due to the complexity of description of the trait. In an attempt to simplify the construct SPS may be best thought of as typified by the DOES acronym.

- *Depth of processing* of all experience and stimuli. A preference for observation and reflection before action and thorough cognitive processing of all experience.
- *Overstimulation in certain highly individualized circumstances.* Though there is no set list of overstimulating events certain sensory stimuli like

noises, smells, strong lighting, intemperate conditions, or exposure to strong interpersonal energy may lead some to many HSPs to feel a need to withdraw and recharge in quiet. *The variability of this aspect of SPS is extreme and must be emphasized, so we do not homogenize an otherwise widely variable trait.* The tendency toward overstimulation is often the only way many people identify with SPS without reading well-researched literature written by credentialed researchers.

- *Emotional responsivity* and *high empathy*. Emotionality serves as the trigger mechanism for SPS with activating events initiating cognitive processing of the experience. High empathy may be present in HSPs, though it is highly individualized and may be context-specific. Emphasizing again the variability of SPS not all HSPs will be deeply empathic in every situation, nor will every event prove to activate an HSPs' emotions. In many cases, the influence of society in dampening down the expression of emotions or empathy will serve to cover up SPS to some degree in many people.
- *Sensitivity to subtleties*. HSPs do not possess extraordinary sensory abilities in the sense organs, rather in the way the stimuli is more thoroughly processed in the brain. HSPs do, however, spend more time attending to visual cues in a scene gathering additional information others might miss and pause to reflect before choosing an action.

Additionally, in my research, it has been established that over 90% of HSPs are likely creative individuals with SPS potentially predisposing HSPs toward creative activities and vocations.[19] Here I define creativity as more than the stereotypical notion of producing an end product or performance to include a broader construct inclusive of innovation, complexity of mind, curiosity, openness to new experience, tolerance of ambiguity, and intense sensibility coupled with emotional passion and heightened aesthetic awareness and appreciation. All people may be creative. It's built into us as human beings but seems to be especially so in the highly sensitive person.

Highly sensitive people are drawn to what can best be described as the helping professions, as well as the creative. HSPs work in all careers, but are concentrated more so in those that directly or indirectly are involved in the overall care and positive growth of other people.[16] HSPs are a diverse segment of the overall population with a marginally rare personality trait living within societal structures that may extend beyond the ancestral environment the trait evolved in thereby potentially constricting preferred behaviors. Many Western societies seem to be liberalizing, which may allow a more natural expression of the trait, though some regions and areas remain more focused on the external life of the individual than a holistic vision of inner and outer.

Sensation seeking in the highly sensitive person

In this book, we approach the discussion of sensation seekers as a subset of the highly sensitive population. Sensation seekers are approximately 30% of the highly sensitive population, which as we know is about 15-20% of the overall total population.[9] Sensation seekers certainly exist who are not highly sensitive. Indeed, sensation seeking and glorification of all things thrilling, adventurous and novel seem to permeate much of Western culture, but how do sensation seeking and sensory processing sensitivity interact in just one person? How does what we term a *sensitive sensation seeker* embody what seems like at least partially contradictory traits? Will one trait dominate the other or will they find balance and an equal expression?

To find the answers to these questions and more I interviewed dozens of HSPs who self-described as sensation seekers. I asked them a variety of questions concerning their early, adult and later lives seeking to uncover the various ways these traits interact and the relative implications for those of us who are sensitive sensation seeker. What I ended up with was quite a dynamic group of creative, fascinating, diverse people who very graciously allowed us to enter their worlds for a moment in time.

As this book unfolds, I suggest that readers refrain from the human tendency to create neat boxes or categories prematurely in which we place our understanding of other people. We are all human beings, that is, members of the species known as Homo sapiens. Some of us happen to be more sensitive than others with some special considerations, but in the end, *we are not so very different.* As we progress through this book, my hope is that I will adequately communicate to you the true vision of complexity that I saw revealed to me through this research.

If we can appreciate our differences, while coming to a deep understanding of who we are, we can be of much benefit to our families, employers, communities, and to the world. It is through appreciating our diversity while honoring the strengths each person expresses, that we may truly embody inclusive, resilient, well-functioning of all members of society at all levels. I am truly in awe of the human potential each person possesses and intend this book as an educational tool through which we may all benefit as we journey together on this voyage of self-discovery and personal growth.

Key Takeaways

- Human behavior is profoundly influenced by social context, but also genetics, and conscious choice.

- The process of natural selection has filtered out traits that did not serve the purposes of survival or reproduction leaving traits that, on average, promoted the reproduction of those who had the trait/s.

- Adaptations are evolved psychological mechanisms that take in a narrow slice of information and make if/then choices based on the traits attributes (approach and check it out or avoid and gather more information while reflecting).

- Personality traits represent possible behaviors and are not absolute guarantors we will act or react a specific way. Every person is different and will react differently in a given context.

- Sensation seeking is a personality trait comprising four main aspects: thrill and adventure seeking, experience and novelty seeking, disinhibition, and boredom susceptibility. Sensation seeking is more heritable than other traits but declines with age except for the boredom susceptibility aspect. Risk-taking is a correlate, but not a primary aspect. Sensation seekers either underestimate the risk or accept the risks involved in a behavior.

Thrill

- Sensory processing sensitivity is a constellation of personality traits: depth of processing (more elaborate processing in the brain) of all stimulation, overstimulation in highly individualized circumstances, emotional responsiveness and high empathy, and sensitivity to subtleties. SPS is present in 15-20% of the overall population and present in at least 100 other species.[20] SPS is not related to sensory processing disorder, nor is it an illness, diagnosis, or absolute. SPS is moderated by early childhood environment, the social environment, and conscious choices.[9]

Questions and Answers

How do I know if I'm a highly sensitive person or a high sensation seeker?

Most of us will have an intuitive sense that we identify with certain aspects of the descriptors of one or both traits, but the best way to know is to take the self-tests. You may find the self-test for sensory processing sensitivity at http://hsperson.com/test/highly-sensitive-test/. The sensation seeking self-test may be found at http://hsperson.com/test/high-sensation-seeking-test.

Ultimately, you should take the self-tests and reflect on which questions you answered as being most true for you. That, along with reading the relevant literature, will help you better understand how one or both traits (and specific aspects within each trait) have influenced your life.

What are the best books on highly sensitive people and sensation seekers?

There are a number of good books and, now, a documentary movie on sensory processing sensitivity. The movie is called *Sensitive-The Untold Story* and is available to rent/buy at https://sensitive-theuntoldstory.vhx.tv/buy/sensitive-the-untold-story-1.

A list of books for <u>sensory processing sensitivity</u> includes:

Elaine Aron – The Highly Sensitive Person.

> The Highly Sensitive Person in Love.
>
> The Highly Sensitive Person's Workbook.
>
> The Highly Sensitive Child: Helping Our Children Thrive When the World Overwhelms Them.
>
> Psychotherapy and the highly sensitive person: Improving outcomes for that minority of people who are the majority of clients.

Ted Zeff – The Strong Sensitive Boy.

> The Power of Sensitivity.
>
> The Highly Sensitive Person's Survival Guide: Essential Skills for Living Well in an Overstimulating World).
>
> The Highly Sensitive Person's Companion: Daily Exercises for Calming Your Senses in an Overstimulating World.

Tracy Cooper – Thrive: The Highly Sensitive Person and Career.

Barrie Jaeger – Making Work Work for the Highly Sensitive Person.

A list of <u>peer-reviewed research papers</u> (for those interested in the hardcore science behind SPS):

Elaine Aron – Sensory processing sensitivity and its relation to introversion and emotionality (Journal of Personality and Social Psychology, issue 73).

Thrill

>Sensory processing sensitivity: A review in the light of the evolution of biological responsivity (Personality and Social Psychology Review, Issue 16).

>The clinical implications of Jung's concept of sensitiveness (Journal of Jungian Theory and Practice, Issue 8).

>The highly sensitive brain: An fMRI study of sensory processing sensitivity and response to others' emotions (Brain and Behavior, Issue 4).

>Revisiting Jung's concept of innate sensitiveness (Journal of Analytical Psychology, Issue 49).

Jay Belsky and **Michael Pluess**

>Beyond diathesis stress: differential susceptibility to environmental influences (Psychological Bulletin, Issue 135).

>Vantage sensitivity: individual differences in response to positive experiences (Psychological Bulletin, Issue 139).

For **sensation seeking** the list includes:

Books

Marvin Zuckerman

>Behavioral expressions and biosocial bases of sensation seeking.

>Sensation seeking and risky behavior.

Peer-reviewed research papers

Marvin Zuckerman

Dimensions of sensation seeking (Journal of consulting and clinical psychology, Issue 36).

Jonathan Roberti

A review of behavioral and biological correlates of sensation seeking (Journal of Research in Personality, Issue 38).

Agnes Norbury and **Masud Husain**

Sensation seeking: dopaminergic modulation and risk for psychopathology (Behavioral Brain Research, Issue 288).

Marcus Munafo, Binnaz Yalcin, Saffron Willis-Owen, and **Jonathan Flint**

Association of the D4 receptor gene (DRD4) and approach-related personality traits: A meta-analysis and new data.

Rick Hoyle, Michael Stephenson, Philip Palmgreen, Elizabeth Lorch, and **R. Donohew**

Reliability and validity of a brief measure of sensation seeking (Personality and Individual Differences, Issue 32).

Chunhui Chen, et al

Contributions of dopamine-related genes and environmental factors to highly sensitive personality: a multi-step neuronal system-level approach (PlosOne, Issue 6).

There are many others, but this list is a great start toward a better understanding of sensory processing sensitivity, sensation seeking and related topics (gender, career, alternative conceptualizations).

Thrill

Part 2

The second part of this book introduces the findings of an extensive qualitative study that was conducted to understand better the lived experiences of 35 high sensation seeking highly sensitive people. The study results are further solidified by the inclusion of results of a survey given to 1,551 highly sensitive people. In this survey, HSPs were asked to answer specific questions regarding sensation seeking preferences. The results are fascinating and offer us a deep look into specific aspects of sensation seeking point by point.

This section of the book is grouped into distinct themes for each chapter with actual quotes from sensitive sensation seekers in the study and analysis of each aspect. To enhance the scope of this book, I have also included a question and answer section at the end of many chapters with real questions that have been asked of me by sensitive sensation seekers in this study and in my consulting practice. The intent of these QA's is to present real world considerations we all have as sensitive sensation seekers.

Lastly, this close examination of the lives of sensitive sensation seekers will prepare us for part three of this book, which will include actual narratives from sensitive sensation seekers in the study.

Chapter 2
Beginning at the Beginning – Childhood

"[Kids] don't remember what you try to teach them. They remember what you are." –Jim Henson, *It's Not Easy Being Green: And Other Things to Consider*

Childhood is a time of great innocence, joy, free expression of creative energies, and easy friendships with other children and many adults, but for many people, childhood is also a time when great emotional damage is inflicted that may affect brain development and future behaviors long-term. In this chapter, we will look at both sides of early childhood experiences (positive and negative) and explore their relative impact on well-functioning throughout the life course.

This book is intended to be primarily descriptive in nature as the first book of its kind detailing the intersection of sensation seeking and sensory processing sensitivity. You may notice variations in your experiences in childhood in the quotations and explanations. I advise readers to spend some time in reflection on the numerous points made in this chapter and *not* think of childhood as inconsequential to future life. As we will see the impact of aversive events, as well as supportive, can be significant in their reach.

Childhood trauma

"My childhood was not a supportive one." In my survey 50% agreed or strongly agreed with this statement.

The role of adverse childhood experiences (ACE's) has been well studied and documented. Among the most prominent ways ACE's may affect our brain development, according to researcher Donna Nakazawa,[21] are:

Epigenetic shifts, in which chemical markers adhering to genes that regulate our stress responses are reset to high (potentially for life).

Size and shape of the brain. ACE's can have an influence on the size of a region of the brain called the hippocampus that regulates the processing of memory, emotions, and stress responses. People with high ACE scores also may have impaired prefrontal cortexes affecting their decision making and self-regulatory abilities and the amygdala, which is the fear-processing center of the brain. Both regions, if underdeveloped, may contribute to our overreacting to even minor stresses in life.

Neural pruning in which cells known as microglial cells that normally perform a housekeeping role in the brain by pruning unneeded cells and absorbing cellular debris instead excrete a neurochemical leading to potentially chronic inflammation (if the person experiences ACE's) that can contribute to mood disorders, poor decision making, and reset the tone of the brain for life.

Telomeres, or the protective caps that sit on the ends of DNA strands. In people with ACE's these caps experience greater erosion thereby opening the body to premature aging and diseases.

Default mode network. This complex tangle of interconnected brain neurocircuitry that stands ready to help us interpret relevant from non-relevant in a given situation is not as active with less connectivity in the network. This connectivity issue may be true even decades later in life as the person experiences difficulty in reacting appropriately to a given situation.

Brain-body pathway. We now know the immune system may flood the brain *and* body with inflammatory chemicals via the lymphatic system. For people with ACE's this inflammation may be chronic leading to increased likelihoods of disease. Overall bodily inflammation is now being implicated as an underlying cause of many disabling diseases.

Brain connectivity. Weaker connections between the prefrontal cortex and the hippocampus (and the amygdala for girls) in people with high ACE's may lead to greater emotional reactivity to everyday events as we overreact to perceived dangers and threats.

This discussion may seem very dire, but to a large degree the brain has incredible plasticity and may be retrained through efforts at self-care, emotion regulation, and reframing of appropriate responses. In some cases, it would be most helpful to work with a skilled therapist knowledgeable about ACE's, sensory processing sensitivity, and sensation seeking. For others, certain medications might assist them in mitigating the effects of depression, anxiety, and mood inconsistencies. We should be mindful that there is a wide variation in moods and emotional reactions to a given situation and not assume we have a disorder requiring *any* intervention. Indeed, sensitive sensation seekers may be deeply complex individuals with a broader possible range of behaviors.

The question may arise for some regarding parenting and ACE's. In particular, if we happen to have a high number of ACE's will we pass them on to our children through our behaviors? You will be pleased to learn that many sensitive sensation seekers eventually have children of their own and make quite wonderful parents raising children free of ACE's, though the effects of our own ACE's may linger throughout life to some degree.

To learn your ACE score, you may visit the following website for a self-test and further explanation: http://www.acestudy.org/ace_score.

Just get over it!

We've heard this familiar refrain from others as they angrily admonish us not to use experiences from long ago as "excuses" for current poor choices. To an extent, there is a grain of truth in not allowing the past to overshadow our current reality and undermine our attempts to find fulfillment, peace, and joy in life. The aforementioned developmental differences in those who have experienced ACEs makes it clear there are real anatomical deficiencies that may be corrected to some degree. If you were told you had a problem that may be deeply influencing your life and the lives of others (our children, mates, or partners) wouldn't you be willing to discuss it seriously?

I understand the desire to bury old hurts deeply and just move on and to some extent, we all do simply move on and age while life continues to happen. The opportunity here is to move beyond anger, repressed sadness and hurt to a point where real healing can begin. Once we are willing to face our authentic selves, including confronting ugly realities about our pasts, then we can begin the process of self-care with the hope of diminishing the amount of anger, hate, and sadness we project out to others.

Is sensation seeking more accepted than sensitivity?

For those readers who have read my previous book, *Thrive: The Highly Sensitive Person and Career*,[22] we know that sensitive children (especially males) are often not supported for expressing sensitivity. Parents often concern themselves with society's arbitrary standards of gender and fear that non-compliance will hurt their child's chances of success and happiness in the world. Parents often may do great damage (sometimes unknowingly) as we attempt to modify a sensitive child's behaviors. But, is the same true for a child exhibiting sensation seeking?

Here again, there seems to be a gender divide with boys being more accepted as daring risk takers charging ahead with no fear, while girls may often be discouraged from doing so. Jessica stated: "I grew up in a time when girls didn't do that stuff. I was considered sort of the tomboy, but it was like "gosh, you shouldn't be on a motorcycle or a skateboard or whatever." They tried to put me in dresses and make a girl, but I just had this aspect that I just wasn't ladylike. Kids now have progressed to a point where society is not so rigid anymore. People are easing up on that."

Interestingly, acceptance of sensation seeking in girls varies from family to family with some girls reporting acceptance for their "uniqueness." This acceptance of sensation seeking in girls would seem to follow the Western cultural trend of strong females engaging in activities not traditionally thought of as feminine. Perhaps again with the liberalization of culture females are returning to a more ancestral mode where a moderate expression of sensation seeking may have been less divided by gender. Eleanor related "generally being a HSP is female and being HSS is male in the American culture. The HSS part of me that gets people going that gets them rallying around I don't think is that hard."

Many Western cultures prize sensation seeking as a personality trait, but not sensitivity, which may be thought of *by some* as neuroticism or being a "difficult" person (by the society). Sensitivity, of course, is a more complex construct that in its totality is quite a *beautiful* personality trait producing creators, thinkers, and healers, not to mention a plethora of other meaningful, productive, essential individuals. Chloe expressed "My parents were less concerned about gender and more about where I was fully expressed. Gender for me is irrelevant. I never let it hold me back." Chloe's parents clearly were supportive of her sensitivity and her sensation seeking: "My childhood was very adventurous. We went skiing, canoeing, hiking. We were a very active family. Everybody in my family was very artistic. We were always doing things of that nature. Being an HSP at home was very natural. It's not until you get to school that you realize how different you are." Realizing that we are somehow different may be most apparent upon entering the school environment where differences are not only obvious but seized on by other children. The role of the parent (and others) modeling supportive behavior cannot be emphasized too much.

Differing parental styles

"The household I grew up in was often chaotic." In my survey 50% agreed or strongly agreed with this statement.

Just as every child is different, every parent is different too in the way parental duties and responsibilities are carried out. Each choice affects the child's experience of early life and influences how he views the world. A parent who is too protective may cause a child to feel fearful, anxious, or to dread new experiences, while a parent who is too lenient may breed a child with no boundaries or sense of consequences for his actions.

Parents as well are on their own individualized life journeys with ups and downs that influence day to day interactions. Though many parents may be very loving and supportive in their lives and to their children others may be less able to embrace the role of parent fully and intentionally, or otherwise cause trauma through household conflict, upheaval, or instability. These ACE's may deeply affect the growth and development of a sensitive sensation seeking child. I have found that it is likely that over 50% of HSPs have experienced ACE's or otherwise been rejected for expressing sensitivity.[18] *That number is likely higher.* Sensation seeking in the highly sensitive child may be more accepted than sensitivity, but we must be careful as parents to honor and respect the gifts of both traits in our children so as not to suppress significant parts of our children's personalities. Suppression of significant parts of our psyches may lead to lifelong internal conflicts as people grapple with how to express and embody who they feel themselves to be.

Parental self-awareness

Raising the sensitive, sensation seeking child may be quite the complex task as we observe our children exhibiting behaviors that we may think of as more desirable within a society, such as curiosity, exploring, or highly physical activities, yet troubling for us as sensitive children may also exhibit a lack of conformity, preference to observe before acting, or who may become easily overstimulated in certain circumstances. The pressures for conformity are enormously strong for all individuals, but none more so than for parents who have so much life energy, time, and intrinsic interest in seeing their progenies succeed within societies. One of the major aspects parents of sensitive, sensation seeking children need to have in place is a deep personal awareness of their personalities and an understanding of the context within which they have chosen to live (or find themselves).

Some parents (even HSPs) may be quite conformist in nature and adhere closely to societal norms regarding behavior, worldview, and expectations. Others are less concerned with maintaining conventions and instead emphasize individualism whereby the needs and desires of the person are paramount. This tendency varies by culture and within cultures. What we need to be aware of as parents is how we are positioned within the society we live in and how that informs the way we choose to parent. If you are an HSP, it is likely you endured some amount of misunderstanding as a child regarding your sensitivity and seek to ensure that does not happen for your child (this certainly was the case for me as I parented my four children). If you are not an HSP, you may feel completely unprepared in parenting the sensitive child.

We now live in a time when good information about how to parent the sensitive child is readily available from experts. A simple internet search will return some useful books offering great advice and insights into workable parenting strategies. I suggest blending this search for knowledge with an overall personal search for self-awareness that may lead you to greater peace and understanding about your propensities and predilections as a parent. None of us are born as parents: we only learn how to parent from a multitude of sources and with long experience. The more you know yourself, the better equipped you will be to manage the stresses and trials of parenting children who are sensitive sensation seekers. These children may be challenging, but they also offer the opportunity to be a positive force in the growth and development of potentially exceptional individuals.

Profile of the high sensation seeking child

Sensation seeking, as a trait, comprises four main aspects: thrill and adventure seeking, experience or novelty seeking, disinhibition and susceptibility for boredom.[7] One need not be high in all four aspects to be a sensation seeker. Rather it is likely that we may find ourselves more closely identifying with one or more aspects than another. One also does not need to be extremely high in any aspect to be considered a sensation seeker. Indeed, most of us who identify as sensation seekers are more likely somewhere in the middle of the bell curve than at the extreme.

The high sensation seeking child might enjoy taking physical risks like jumping off of chairs (or other heights), riding bicycles at high speed, or other activities that provide a physical "rush." Though the intent is to experience the "rush" sensation seekers are willing to take the risks involved to have the experience. The sensation seeking child might be very interested in new or novel experiences and thrive on trips to art museums, music concerts, or exploring on her own. Though there may be less risk involved (and gladly for the parent) the "rush" from experiencing a new place or event is no less enjoyable for the sensation-seeking child.

You might ask "how does disinhibition factor into a child's life, isn't that more for adults?" Disinhibition, or the willingness to step outside of normal personal and societal boundaries, may be present in any person at any age. All parents will acknowledge that children often do things they are not "supposed" to just because it's interesting, fun, or to test boundaries. In the sensation seeking child, disinhibition may be even stronger leading to underestimating the risks involved in an activity. Disinhibition may serve as a trigger for seeking thrills or new experiences. A susceptibility for boredom may also serve as a trigger mechanism propelling a child toward seeking new experiences (novelty) or thrills.

Profile of the highly sensitive child

Sensory processing sensitivity is a trait marked by four main dimensions: depth of processing of all sensations and experiences, a tendency toward overstimulation in certain circumstances, high empathy and emotional responsiveness, and sensitivity to subtle stimuli or visual (or other) cues.[12]

The highly sensitive child may feel things more deeply than other children; prefer to reflect or think before taking action; feel things very deeply and be affected very deeply when things happen; be very empathic toward animals or other people; exhibit quick emotions; pick up on subtle cues others miss (like noticing an interesting shape in the clouds, a smell that is faint, or a noise in the background); and tire in stimulating environments before others.[16]

Sensitive children differ from other children in their sheer complexity and range of possible behaviors. A sensitive child may be quiet, observant, and seemingly "not there," but nothing could be further from the truth. The sensitive child absorbs everything happening around him and needs time and space to process all of the stimulation. Other sensitive children may be quite sociable and indistinguishable from other children except that they may tire of the social interactions or stimulation before others and need to recharge in quiet. The more extraverted sensitive child will still exhibit the same depth of processing of all stimulation, high empathy, emotional responsiveness, and sensitivity to subtleties, but differ in their outward expressions of sociability.

Before we move to examining the intersection of both traits in sensitive sensation seeking children let's look at several quotes:

Thrill

"I was always very adventurous as a kid. I used to collect rocks and things and all types of inanimate objects and keep them in my room all tucked in because I worried they weren't going to be happy. I'd worry about the happiness of everything in the world. It was odd and took a long time to get out of that." –Claire

"I was very bright in school. I was always social and in the good readers club. I had friends. I didn't think of myself as different until I was 16. My father was usually drunk; my mother worked full time. I'm deducing that I wasn't nourished very much when I was young because of those two factors. One telling story is once two black kids chased me home from school and I ran into my house, and my Dad threw me back out onto the sidewalk. I was kind of on my own. I was severely abused as a child." –Danny

"I had one of those fairly classic troubled childhoods. Lots of emotional issues raised by fairly narcissist parents. My Dad experienced a great deal of depression, and I was very close to him, so it was very intense for me too. I also had a large amount of bullying and moved around a great bit in my primary schools. I was quite conflicted in an intuitive sense between my shyness and sensitivity and needed stimulation. I remember quite often feeling torn. I needed that level of stimulation and sought out the various buzzes in certain forms like music. It wasn't very satisfying, and I felt quite torn. I had a really high level of awareness, understanding it intuitively. I used to spend my entire lunchtime with headphones, so I could engage in that intensity of the music and protect myself otherwise. " – Robyn

"School was terrible...I didn't realize what it was at the time, but it was the noise, the smells, the lights, the people, just everything. I was just constantly overwhelmed, and I was a straight A student when I could handle it. I realized

in kindergarten that I was different from other students. Everybody took all the toys away from me because I was the shy kid. I hated it because it drew all the attention to me." –Eleanor

"I was very culturally thwarted by growing up in Dallas. My mother, however, supported my sense of social justice and honored my questions, even if she couldn't answer them. I just knew the external world mirrored back to us that something was wrong with us. I was always angry about it. I had this sense there was nothing wrong with us there was something wrong with the external world. Maybe I got that from my mother's unconditional love. It was a source of strength." –Jacquelyn

Being a "source of strength" is a key aspect of raising children that are less anxious, more willing to venture out into the world and try new experiences, and build their identities on a firm foundation of love and support. We can aid this process by truly knowing *ourselves*, the context of which we have chosen to live, and our strengths and weaknesses as individuals.

Profile of the high sensation seeking highly sensitive child

"My parents were supportive of my sensitivity when I was growing up." In my survey 61% disagreed or strongly disagreed with this statement.

The child who has both personality traits is quite a complex individual indeed. Though sensation seeking and sensory processing sensitivity might seem like diametrically opposed traits, there are some important ways they overlap. Understanding these overlaps is important to understanding how the traits interact, manifest and struggle to coexist in one person.

Thrill

Thrill and adventure seeking, though portrayed as a preference for extreme sports or physical thrills, may be more moderate with children seeking safer thrills like carnival rides that feel less risky or abrupt, rollerblading, or cruising down a slide at the park. Sensitive children who are also sensation seekers will likely experience even milder thrills more intensely. For the sensitive child, it's the *intensity* of the experience that is thrilling, even if the overall adventure may seem less so to others. As Claire stated: *"I like to go cliff-climbing and look for fossils in the ravine. It's kind of one of my riskier things I do because it is quite a steep dive. I like the feeling and thrill of it. I also seek out horror movies because I don't get scared easily. I try and seek it out because it's a unique feeling or me. I love being thrilled, on the edge...I seek out thrills to get a big feeling in."*

Getting that "big feeling in" was mirrored by Jessica's sensation seeking behaviors mixed with her sensitivity *"I was a real daredevil and people could not understand how I could be so withdrawn and do such crazy things. I was a huge rollercoaster junkie and we used to make these tree swings and swing out over two 30 foot deep ravines. I dirt bike rode, I climbed trees; I was really a big paradox. No one could really wrap their mind around me growing up."* The sensation seeking sensitive child may indeed represent a paradox to parents who cannot relate to the adrenaline rush that is experienced with thrill and adventure seeking. Perhaps more accessible for some is another aspect of sensation seeking.

Experience and novelty seeking is probably the biggest crossover aspect between sensation seeking and high sensitivity with curiosity and a preference for new experiences occupying a position of prominence in such children. The sensitive sensation seeking child may or may not prefer a structured activity (like a trip to an art museum complete with a guide). Instead, she may prefer to wander freely through the galleries absorbing and experiencing the nuances of color and mood in the artwork *and* in the other people around her. Indeed the sensitive, sensation seeking child may be a keen people watcher and enjoy the wide variety of individuals.

Disinhibition in the sensitive, sensation seeking child may be less of a factor as the reflective proclivity serves a cautionary function probably dampening down the willingness to take undue risks in some children. In this sense the sensitive, sensation seeking child may be pulled in two directions at once: deeply desiring to jump out of the tree with his friends, yet terrified at the same time considering all of the possible consequences (breaking a bone, pain, the humiliation of not looking cool to friends). Disinhibition though may also factor into the sensitive child's desire to explore and experience new things.

"I am easily bored." In my survey 39% agreed or strongly agreed with this statement.

Susceptibility for boredom seems to be a strong issue for sensitive children and sensation seeking children. In the child who is both the need to keep ahead of boredom may be quite strong and he may go to great lengths to avoid boring activities or situations. Many children will recite the familiar "I'm so bored!" refrain, but in the sensitive, sensation seeking child the experience of boredom is almost painful. Boredom is an aversive state that, interestingly, is cast in a negative light in many Western societies where to say one is bored is to admit a personal "weakness."

"I do not like to explore." In my survey 79% disagreed or strongly disagreed with this statement.

Thrill

Fundamentally, boredom may be situational (engaging in a task that is repetitive, lacking intrinsic interest, or does not provide enough stimulation), or dispositional (the child is prone to boredom because of personality traits). In that sense, boredom is a complex construct that goes beyond the notion that each of us is entirely responsible for maintaining our optimal level of motivation in monotonous, repetitive, uninteresting activities or circumstances. Sensitive sensation seeking children may not be as skilled as adults in managing boredom as they wrestle with strong impulses to explore and do interesting, fun activities or be around others who provide the range of stimulation they find most appropriate. Of the four aspects of sensation seeking susceptibility for boredom tends to remain with us the strongest as we progress through the life course.[7]

The supportive childhood

We have covered the lingering effects of adverse childhood events, but what about the childhood that was supportive, happy, and relatively trauma-free? Though no childhood is entirely trauma-free, the determining factor in how ACE's affected us is how deeply we experienced the event. For the sensitive child, an event need not be at the extreme end of trauma to be quite intense and memorable. Sensitive children feel and process stimulation more deeply than those without the trait. Similarly, for those children who are sensitive and sensation seeking the effects of a positive early environment may be profound and energizing.

The effects of having a supportive childhood are well-known and documented in the research. I noted a number of quotes from sensitive sensation seekers expressing how important early support was to their future willingness and ability to venture out into the world, take on new tasks with confidence, and experience less overall anxiety, depression, and isolation.

"One of the benefits of the way I grew up was I was really in charge of my stimulation so while my other friends were taking ballet and music lessons or being in Girls Scouts I was left at home playing imaginary games and keeping myself occupied. I remember hanging wet sheets, we didn't have a washer or dryer so did our laundry at a laundromat, and I would stay in these sheets (it was very hot in summer) and look up at the clouds or daydream and when I got done resting I would want to do something exciting so I would ride my imaginary horse Trigger and I would ride him like really fast all over the neighborhood. Later, when I got a bicycle I would always sneak down to the curvy roads and ride them because it was exciting." – Jacquelyn

"I was very shy. I was very much a loner, very happy like that, but had a very supportive mother who accepted me and supported it. I was very lucky in that respect." – Eleanor

"There was a long sloping street in the town where I grew up that went downhill for probably a mile. I used to ride my ten-speed bike to the top and then ride downhill as fast I could go! I'd be in tenth gear halfway through and probably hitting some crazy speed, but what a rush! I loved it! My Dad, I think understood my need to get those physical thrills in, my Mom, not so much." –Matt

"We lived in a place that I could explore a lot so that was great, and I had a lot of great relationships too that I savor now looking back. My parents didn't put high expectations as far as you have to be this or that. They were very open to what kind of career I wanted to go into. They didn't say you had to go down this road, which was great." –Bruce

Thrill

" I was lucky enough to have a supportive family. I mean it could have gone a whole different way for me. My parents always validated how I felt and encouraged me to listen to my feelings and to listen to my gut instinct. It was really empowering for me as a child. I am so grateful I had intuitive, sensitive grandparents and intuitive, sensitive parents because I think it would have been very difficult otherwise. I think of them as gifts." –Taylor

The Value of Free Play

One of the recurring patterns that arise in supportive childhoods is the way children are allowed to explore freely and play on their own. Having the opportunity to explore freely, encounter problems, and conceptualize solutions imparts an internal locus of control. Feeling like we can master the challenges put before us is essential if we are expected to be able to function in a world strewn with challenges.

Free play allows the child a chance to indulge the thrill and adventure seeking, and experience and novelty seeking that are so endemic to many children, but especially the sensitive sensation seeker. I was such a child myself growing up in the 1970s in small-town Missouri where our neighborhood group of kids freely explored, played, and endlessly entertained ourselves. I cannot say this freedom was a conscious effort on the part of parents then; rather they knew intrinsically that free play had value, and perhaps it was easier and simpler than constantly overseeing their children's range of activities or involving them in a constant stream of adult led activities.

I want to emphasize this point: *free play allows the sensitive sensation seeking child a chance to explore, encounter the world, and learn to rely on themselves for solutions and develop an internal sense of mastery over challenges.* Without free play children are more prone to anxiety, fear, and depression because the challenges they inevitably will encounter will indeed seem frightening and they will lack the confidence and self-efficacy that they can effect a positive outcome. Free play is one very important thing that supportive parents do, and it does not depend on socioeconomic status or imply a lack of caring or abdication of parental responsibility. We obviously should take care to guarantee the safety of our children in the immediate environment.

It would be great if we all had entirely supportive childhoods where our true natures were encouraged, and we were each supported in becoming our highest and truest selves, but many of us (the author included) had early childhoods that were fine, but later experienced trauma, conflict, abuse, or neglect. Jessica related to me how her childhood had been "very chaotic," but that her mother's decision to enroll her in a private school was probably her "saving grace." As Jessica continued: *"The lady who ran this school was very plugged into her students. She was a very strict taskmaster, but very fair, and I blossomed under that structure. When I tested into the school, she said to my mom "Do you realize this child is gifted?"*

The issue of giftedness and the sensitive sensation seeking child came up before in previous studies, and I was careful to ask each person whether they had been identified as gifted in childhood. The results? About half identified as gifted, which is interesting again and denotes that sensation seekers (even gifted ones) may be more likely to volunteer for studies they feel excited by (novelty and new experiences).

The benefits of structure

Thrill

Jessica's story also suggests the role that structure may play in helping sensitive sensation seeking children channel their energies into productive avenues. In fact, the role that structure can play in providing a framework within which children can receive support, nurturing, and a reliably predictable core set of activities (classes at school, chores at home, etc…) may augment or substitute for an otherwise deficient or marginal environment. Sensitive sensation seeking children may prize their autonomy and need to follow their passions at the moment, but may benefit from a certain amount of structure that can provide a disciplined framework within which to function that will serve them well throughout life.

Types of sensation seekers

Impulsive and unsocialized

Zuckerman has proposed that there are two types of sensation seekers. The first is the impulsive, unsocialized individual for whom sensation seeking is not tempered by an accompanying cautionary instinct. Researchers suggest that impulsive, unsocialized sensation seeking may include the disinhibition, boredom susceptibility, and experience seeking aspects potentially implying "less sensitivity to risk, a lack of planning skills, increased hostility, negative emotions, and anger…and may be conniving, non-conforming, and non-conventional."[8]

For such children, their impulsivity leads them to take undue risks on spur of the moment choices. The unsocialized aspect is especially hazardous when combined with impulsivity because the thrills can include activities like fighting, stealing, taking illicit drugs, drinking alcohol, engaging in risky, unprotected sex with random partners, or causing harm to others.[8] In the sensitive sensation seeking child this may be mitigated to some extent by sensitivity, which may cause a child to be less impulsive and consider the consequences before acting, but the implications for society in terms of unrealized potential, harm to others, and misery are too great.

As parents, we each need to ask ourselves if we are acting as good role models for our children *and others*. Many children today are not able to look up to adults in the public eye as exemplars of positive behaviors with a moral compass. It's up to each of us to be *that* parent who other kids can admire and emulate as they construct their lives. Stand up and be counted parents! Volunteer to coach sports teams, lead children's reading groups or otherwise serve as community anchors around which the youth may learn what appropriate adult behavior and morals look like. Our communities are exactly what we make them.

Non-impulsive and socialized

Non-impulsive sensation seeking may be more positive and includes the thrill and adventure seeking aspect of sensation seeking. I suggest the experience and novelty seeking aspect may also be quite positive as it may entail curiosity, openness, and growth opportunities. I should clarify that many of the activities we engage in as sensation seekers are often impulsive in nature. The difference is the planning tends to be more considerate of the risks, and the activities tend not to harm others in any way. Being socialized implies a certain respect and concern for others weighing our actions based on acceptable/unacceptable as we have learned from the culture.

Earlier we said that impulsive, unsocialized children might be non-conforming and non-conventional. That is true and does represent a type of antisocial non-conformity that may be harmful to society, but simply *being non-conforming and non-conventional is an attribute we all share as sensitive sensation seekers.* Zuckerman states that we "dance to the beat of a different drummer...searching for the novel experience...seeking out that which is different."[7] If your child is non-conventional and non-conforming, it may worry you a great deal! Rest assured, though that, if we have done our jobs as parents, by which I mean if we have provided a supportive, prosocial, accepting, loving home while our children were young, it's likely that our children will be fine as adults. They may or may not fit our vision of what we wish them to be (especially if we have suffered on our journeys), but we have to learn that each person's path in life is different and honor their choices trusting they will be fully capable of making good choices.

The forms that sensation seeking and sensitivity take are probably determined by the overall environment with socioeconomic class filtering the ways children learn to express their sensitivity and their sensation seeking. There is a great deal of variation in the types of activities afforded to upper class (even middle class) families compared to those from the lower or under classes. Though we can debate exactly where one class ends and another begins there are significant differences regarding education, parenting, and household culture that encourage prosocial behavior, neutral, or even antisocial behavior.

Education

What about the education of the sensitive sensation seeking child? For the non-impulsive, socialized sensitive sensation seeking child what would work best would likely be a mix of activities and styles that both promote calm, yet allow for exciting activities at other times. The sensitive sensation seeker is a complex person who may alternately need his quiet time away from everything and everyone and later is ready for adventures and exploration.

Sensitive sensation seeking children thrive on a mixture of free play and structure.

Sensitive sensation seeking children require more autonomy than do others. We thrive on following that "different drummer" Zuckerman mentioned, but too much unfocused activity may be counterproductive. Providing a structure helps us to discipline our energies and feel some security in knowing what is expected of us. The type of structure provided to sensitive sensation seeking children shouldn't be too rigid or dogmatic, but it should provide opportunities for challenging tasks that allow for the growth of the child (flow activities, in short, more about these later).

In both traits creativity is common with high sensation seekers tending to do better in open-ended problem solving.[7] This is further aided by the often strong intuition of the sensitive side, which often makes connections before more linear thinkers can reason a problem out. Both traits are also rooted in an openness to new experience.[7] [9] This openness allows for the accumulation of new information on a continual basis. Openness also predisposes us to what some of us have termed *"fascinations."*

Fascinations

Many of the sensitive sensation seekers in this study expressed how they have always found themselves deeply fascinated by a topic during which time they would deeply explore it using every available medium until they

Thrill

had exhausted their interest, then they move on just as quickly to the next topic. When I was a teen, I recall being interested in the ancient Egyptians, space travel, and the history of warfare all within one short period! Later I became fascinated by fine art, gardening, house building, and landscape architecture (in addition to architecture). *This infatuation with topics for varying periods of time is completely normal for the sensitive sensation seeking child!* Please do not leap to the conclusion that your child may have ADHD or lacks scholarly ability. Your child has simply followed her nose to the things that interest her most: indulge that!

"I realized how sometimes my fascinations scare people. It scares people because they are not as deeply involved in the things I'm talking about so what I'm presenting is so complex their self-belief about whether they are smart enough to keep up comes up, and they don't want to lose face." –Prisha

"It's been my ability to focus very intently on a topic that fascinates me that has, cumulatively, added up to me being very broad-based and knowledgeable about a range of sometimes obscure topics." –Matt

"I think the biggest with high sensation seeking and high sensitivity is you have more creativity. It's like these bursts of innovation and growth. I find with these people there's a certain open-mindedness that a lot of other people don't have." –Claire

The sensitive sensation seeking child is apt to have a very rich inner life, enjoy spending time in exploring things, places, and people, and alternate between needing some down time to recharge and opportunities to push their boundaries. Sensitive sensation seeking children may be significantly damaged in childhood if they are in unsupportive environments. Unsocialized, almost antisocial, impulsivity and resulting behaviors may result from chaotic, abusive, or neglectful situations. However, the opposite is true for supportive environments with children benefitting tremendously from understanding, nurturing, and caring parenting. This supportive environment may be true, of course, for any child, but more so for the sensitive sensation seeker due to the more elaborate processing of experience and more deeply felt aspects of emotion. As we will learn in subsequent chapters, the potential is great for those of us who learn love, caring, and acceptance.

Questions and Answers

My childhood was fairly traumatic with episodes of domestic violence, abuse, and neglect. I also tested high in ACE's. Can I recover from this poor early start in life?

First, it is scary to see the number of ACE's any of us may have. The important thing to note is that recovery from Adverse Childhood Experiences is possible, but it will take a good deal of effort on your part to work through the issues you may have as a result of these experiences. Skilled therapists may be able to help you work through some of the most severe issues, while others may soften in tone and intensity as you age. The important thing is to be aware of how our ACE's may still be impacting our lives and work to mitigate their influence.

My child seems to be adventurous and likes thrills, but is also cautious and seems not to take undue risks. Should I push her to be less concerned with risk and go for it for the sake of having the experience?

Assessing the relative risk in an activity is an important skill to possess. Children who are cautious may simply be calculating risk versus reward and feeling anxiety about the experience. Though we may wish our children to have new experiences (ones we think of as desirable as adults) it may be better for sensitive children to be allowed to find activities they find enjoyable and be supported in their choices. The more parents model non-judgmental support for a sensitive child the more likely it may be that a child is willing to venture out and have new experiences. Peer pressure will eventually lead them to new experiences all on their own.

My child seems to be a sensitive, sensation seeker, but in my culture sensitivity is not valued. Should I discourage her sensitivity for the more culturally-accepted/promoted sensation seeking?

A child who is both sensitive and sensation seeking is a complex individual who should not be discouraged from expressing a significant part of herself. People are more whole and healthy when they are encouraged to embrace who they are and find ways to express that in positive ways in the world. Though the powers of conformity are quite strong in groups it is important that we, as parents, encourage and support our children as they grow and develop even if that makes us uncomfortable for a time.

I feel like I need to watch over my children's activities to ensure their safety and vet the friends they choose. Free play, to me, means I have to give up control as a parent?

Not at all. Free play simply means that your child is allowed to choose their activities and begin to make personal choices. Learning to make choices and be responsible for the consequences is an enormously important skill to have. Your child will not always be under your supervision. She will eventually need to decide for herself which friends and activities feel appropriate for her. All of this might seem like you are handing over control, but our role as parents is to mentor, not control. If we set good examples of freely exploring the world, making good choices about activities and friendships we involve ourselves in, and exhibit our internal locus of control it is much more likely that example will be transmitted to our children. Of course, this does not mean we allow our children to engage in activities we know to be unsafe, dangerous, or associate with unsafe individuals. It's about striking a better balance between free play and wise action on the part of the parent.

Key Takeaways

- Childhood experiences of support/non-support may deeply influence how sensitivity and sensation seeking are ultimately expressed in each child. The damages are not irreversible, but remediation may require significant lifelong efforts.
- Parents should be aware of the social context they live in and make choices based on fully supporting their children rather than blindly following social conventions regarding acceptable traits.
- Sensitive sensation seeking children should be allowed a great deal of free play to indulge their need to explore, build self-confidence, and engage their creativity.
- It is normal for sensitive sensation seeking children to exhibit different behaviors than children without the traits. Non-conforming and non-conventional behaviors and interests are seemingly innate to both traits.
- Sensitive sensation seeking children may develop *fascinations* with a topic and wish to explore it

Thrill

deeply. Encourage and support these "deep dives" because they will likely be lifelong patterns and you have an opportunity now to help your children develop effective research skills.

Chapter 3
Career

"What lies behind you and what lies in front of you, pales in comparison to what lies inside of you." –Ralph Waldo Emerson

The work that we do should be work that we love, but often finding the right balance between meaningfulness, autonomy, challenge, interpersonal harmony, and competency in one workplace may be a difficult task. This is especially true for sensitive, sensation seekers who embody two distinct, yet seemingly opposing personality traits whereby the need for new, novel stimulation and experiences may be at odds with a commiserate need for deep thinking, careful planning, and relatively low stimulation environments and interpersonal situations.

In this chapter, we will begin to unpack this deeply complex area of life. Career is such a complex facet of life I devoted the entire book: *Thrive: The Highly Sensitive Person and Career*, to this topic. Now we encounter a subset of the sensitive population: the sensation seeker. This tremendously complex individual embodies all that the sensitive person does plus additional drives to experience thrills/adventures, and new and novel stimulation.

Here I differentiate the sensitive, sensation seeker from the sensitive person in the respect that thrill and adventure seeking and disinhibition (with the associated risk-taking) do not seem to play as significant a role in the lives of sensitive people. I do want to emphasize though that sensitive, sensation seekers share all of the concerns and potentialities of the sensitive person. We are not so very different in the end, but there are some distinct needs that must be acknowledged if we are to examine adequately the one-third of sensitive people who are also sensation seekers. I have broken up our discussion into two parts: career difficulties, where we will look at a number of challenges as expressed by sensitive sensation seekers, and career opportunities, where we will look at some of the major gifts the two traits offer that may lead to viable career paths.

It is important to emphasize here that there is no one "right" career for anyone including sensitive sensation seekers. We are all unique individuals with different talents and abilities influenced by our culture, educational attainment, life choices, and worldviews. Additionally, what works for us at 20 may not work at 30, 40, 50, or beyond. The issue of career is a complex, context-dependent conflagration of decisions made by us and for us. Some things are within our control (like our ability to train for a new job or move to a new area), while others are not (the status of the economy at any given time or economic events that may take place like layoffs or downsizing). Additionally, the external context (society) is constantly undergoing negotiation by each of us as we decide for ourselves the values we will live by. Modern workplaces often hold little, if any, loyalty to conscientious, dedicated workers (though there are exceptions). Moreover, there are some unique challenges for sensitive sensation seekers.

Career challenges

"*I have a need to work on new projects.*" In my survey 66% agreed or strongly agreed with this statement.

Empathy

Career

Sensory processing sensitivity comprises four main core features or aspects: Depth of processing of all experience in the brain (more elaborate processing than in those without the trait), overstimulation in certain, highly individualized circumstances (no two HSPs are alike), high empathy and emotional responsiveness, and sensitivity to subtle stimuli (more time spent studying a visual scene for instance). Here we focus on empathy in the workplace because it is such a prominent experience for the sensitive sensation seekers in my study.

"The highly sensitive side finds people a little bit frightening. When my Mom used to hug me, I felt like my skin was on fire. I didn't like her too close to me or anything. That happens with strangers too. I can feel them when they're too close. That high sensitivity just picks up on people's moods, and I take it wrongly as they are against me. I can feel people a mile away, and no one can sneak up on me. I've heard it is common for HSPs to be startled easily, but not for me." –Claire

"I am very driven, and I feel that my intensity comes from sensation seeking, but my success comes from one-on-one spaces. I was never very successful in community work with large groups of people. I was never able to apply it in that way. I'm not that well suited to it. In groups of ten or more, I'm uncomfortable and in less of a dominant role. I really enjoy the balance of working with people one on one. I have a lot of skills in working one on one with people and it's very satisfying." –Robyn

"I recently got my insurance broker license, but I don't do any brokering at all. I'm like the proofreader of the insurance documentation. It's tough because customers call you up and are irate wanting to know why their premiums went up. You explain once, twice, three times why their premiums increased. I cannot do it because I

would snap. They know I have a bit of a short fuse. I just can't handle stupidity." –Stephanie

"There are certain situations I am fine in and others I just want to hide. I feel exhausted, I feel drained, and I just want to sleep. Face to face communication is best for me because I can read people's faces and body language. I have terrible phone anxiety because it's like being blind. I'm so used to using the full range of what I have that I don't feel I can use that full range when I'm talking on the phone." –Jessica

"We are the ones that deal with a lot of people in these groups, and you are taking on all their energy. You really have to work hard to protect yourself because you will absorb a lot of poison. You are dealing with people who are victims of sexual abuse, physical abuse and trauma, and just a whole manner of issues. It just eventually felt like I had been a combat veteran and I had just seen too much." –Joshua

The workplace is an interpersonally intensive environment for most people. There are respites (breaks) and lull times that soften the intensity, but many positions can be extraordinarily draining for sensitive sensation seekers. Because we experience emotions more intensely, including those projected from others, we are constantly negotiating a balance between feeling, processing, and interpreting the emotion. In some cases, the emotions are not our own, but we must process them simply because we are in a space where conflicts arise.

"I seem to be affected more deeply than others by negative people at work." In my survey 93% agreed or strongly agreed with this statement.

Anyone might be deeply affected by a negative interaction at work, but for the sensitive person, the negativity is processed more deeply both in the brain and body. The cumulative effect of absorbing a strong daily dose of negativity may be more than many sensitive sensation seekers are willing to bear.

"One of the things I struggle with is whether I have lived up to my full potential. Career wise I can't keep a job. I become so overstimulated that I can't go to work, I can't show up. I was doing a lot of jobs dealing with many people. If I had worked in a toll booth, I might have been fine. I was a stripper for a while. Looking back it was a controlled environment, I had a certain level of conversation with interesting people, I got to dance topless, and it filled that need for the adrenaline. I did that for five years and was very good at it. People just enjoyed talking to me. It was like hanging out with friends for an hour or so then they went home. I never felt overstimulated by it. I've never found anything like it that I've been able to move into and feel that much control over my environment." –Jessica

Control over one's environment is a key aspect of balance for any sensitive sensation seeker as we encounter new and unfamiliar situations that may present themselves. The corporate culture may also play a role in undermining our energetic balance: *"Sometimes I really struggle with corporate think: lack of long term planning or busy work and it's a real struggle to be who I am in that environment, and that's why I think I'm not going to be there forever. I think HSPs can't stay in that; you can't survive for long before you feel like you're losing your soul and you have to find a place that supports you."* –Chloe

Energies come from every direction in a working environment including from the corporate structure itself as it periodically asserts its unique cultural beliefs and worldviews to its employees. When we find ourselves at odds with these views the overall environment may be draining. This situation is an enormous problem because most employees typically have little influence over corporate cultures. They can learn to ignore the drivers of "good corporate behavior," probably through alienating themselves, so they don't feel it, or allow it to drain them energetically until they feel they have to escape, but this is not a desirable way to live.

The question arises: Is the sensitive sensation seeker as empathic as the sensitive person? There probably isn't any significant difference unless a sensitive sensation seeker is particularly lower in sensitivity or has learned to "shut out" or exclude certain feelings of empathy. Otherwise, the sensitive sensation seeker experiences the same challenges with absorbing too much energy at once or energies that are negative and draining. The drive to experience new and novel stimulation coupled with boredom susceptibility may mean that sensitive sensation seekers may be less tolerant of negatively stimulating environments. The drive to avoid boredom is extremely strong in many sensitive sensation seekers and may manifest as impatience or disinterest when, in effect, the individual may simply feel a need to protect himself energetically.

Empathy as an advantage

Empathy is always a double-edged sword for those who are high in the trait. Absorb too much negative energy and we will find ourselves drained, frustrated, overwhelmed, and probably in need of a period of quiet to recharge and clear ourselves. On the other hand, empathy is a wonderful trait that allows us to enter the experiences and feelings of other people. We are just as profoundly affected by positive interactions as negative ones and derive great benefit from positive energies. The utility of empathy in the workplace is tremendous.

"I'm good at reading people and applying that to the project. I always get told it's weird that I always know what people are thinking. I think it's something HSPs should be more valued for. I think it's a pretty unique power to have." – Claire

"I was working in psychiatry for a while and had to deal with this patient who was very upset. I had to calm her down, and I thought I would be very exhausted afterward, but I wasn't, I felt like "Wow! This is what I want to do!" I feel like humans are the most interesting thing I can do. I am always studying like psychology, how the mind works. Now I am working with people who have developmental disabilities, and it's a calm work environment because you have to be calm because some of the people are very sensitive to stress. Each and every one is unique, and you have to pick up on the signals." –Freja

"Face to face communication is best for me because I can read people's faces and body language." –Jessica

Empathy as a survival adaptation likely served us well in the past enabling us to "read" other people's visual and emotional cues as to their mental/emotional status at any given time. On a simple threat/non-threat basis empathy keeps us safe, but more deeply empathy alerts us to the suffering of others. Many empathic people work in what we can broadly term the helping professions (healthcare, counseling, education), but empathy across the board is a useful ability to have because we live in deeply complex interpersonal environments where knowing how another person is thinking and feeling may be key to effectively influencing their behaviors or avoiding escalations of emotion.

Salespersons use cues from body language and affect to tailor their sales pitch when we are buying a car.

Thrill

Other sales and customer-oriented positions use empathy as an integral component lessening the psychological distance between the customer and ourselves. As a technical support specialist, I found that my ability to listen to what a client was expressing and project back the fact that I cared and identified with their struggles (mainly software related) went a very long way toward deescalating tensions and moving customers towards their goals. Empathy is a tremendous asset to have when dealing with other people, and it is stunning how far away from anything even resembling empathy many people have strayed in the workplace and beyond.

Boredom susceptibility

Struggles with boredom susceptibility were mentioned more frequently than almost any other issue. Boredom, as described before, is an aversive state whereby we may feel unmotivated, understimulated, or experience a feeling of apathy. A distinct definition of boredom is difficult because researchers over the years have not been able to agree about the complex states (moods and feelings) involved in what we describe as boredom. For our purposes we will rely on a synthesis of boredom as one that is possibly chronic or responsive; agitated versus apathetic; and, further, as suggested by Geiwitz's research suggesting four factors: involves constraint, unpleasantness, low arousal, and repetitiveness.[23]

Boredom susceptibility was described by many sensitive sensation seekers as their "worst enemy."

"Once I have done something for six months it's boring, and I need to move on. I've worked my way up from adjunct to a senior position, and I'm bored out of my mind. If I could never work again, I'd never be bored again. Too many things that I love doing. The reason I'm doing my Ph.D. is

because my job is so boring. The reason I wrote a proposal is the boredom. I need the stimulation. It's finding that other component. Risk taking for some HSPs may be just going out in the world, but that doesn't necessarily fit HSS. Whenever you take on a new job, there's all this new stuff, but within six months it's gone, and I'm bored, and I'll just quit my job and move to another country, which I have done. It was all boredom, and my job, and I think I was trying to run away from it. It didn't work; it followed me." – Eleanor

"I'm always doing something. If I don't feel like I'm doing something, adding something to the world I feel bored." – Claire

"Anything I consider busywork I just do it enough, so I don't get in trouble, then do something else. I learned to play the game, like if the assignment was to read then take a test I did it fast so I could study something else." –Chloe

"I have often chosen stimulation over my sensitivities. Being stimulated has always been very important to me. I'm very easily bored by a lot of things, and I need that stimulation. I certainly think I have a tendency toward boredom. It's been reasonably significant as a motivator especially in career. I rarely just had one job. I need to have multiple projects ongoing." –Robyn

"Boredom is my worst enemy. I have had these jobs where I am like if I am bored I just go to them and say I am so sorry sometimes I would say I was offered another job, but if it is boredom I can't do it. Overstimulation and boredom are two really huge things for me." –Taylor

"I think a full-time job where I had to be there a certain amount of hours; that's not really my thing in the long run. This that I do now that really excites me, that really

intrigues me, if it would be 100% of my work time would maybe be too much. My ideal thing would be doing this thing I'm really passionate about for two days, then one day off. Also having the possibility to go really deep into a project if I feel like doing that." –Freja

Feelings of constraint seem to be a major theme in the above quotes with descriptions of feelings of boredom coming after mastery of a position or as a constant state wherein the person feels a strong drive to remain within an optimal range of arousal. Concurrent with constraint is an implied need for autonomy or self-action. The need for autonomy is well known within the research community as a basic human need, but for sensitive sensation seekers, the need for autonomous self-action seems to be a fundamental driver of behavior (including career choices) that may serve to help people "keep ahead" of boredom.[24]

Repetitive work also seems to produce a great deal of boredom as arousal levels fall and people enter sleeplike states. Productivity falls and distractions (any distractions) may provide a lifeline to consciousness. The number of hours lost to distractions, whether it be surfing the internet, sending and receiving text messages, or otherwise engaging in non-task related activities is enormous.

Short-term projects

There are no easy answers to the problem of boredom, but there is understanding, and that realization can and should be a gateway to each of us being able to label how we are feeling and why. As complex individuals, sensitive sensation seekers embody deep, quick emotions, energy that may come in bursts, and the ever-present propensity for boredom that stalks us like a wolf. Many people have expressed their eventual realization that they are best suited to short-term projects such as Bruce: *"I found I was very project oriented, so I liked having a clear beginning and end of things and then move on to the next thing... projects work well because I don't get bored with it, and I can continue something, and there is a beginning and an end to it."*

The short-term project is beneficial in a number of ways: keeps boredom to a minimum by short duration; accommodates bursts of creative energy; allows for time and space between projects for self-care, and it may help build and sustain personal confidence as one accomplishes a greater number of tasks compared to just one. This may seem elementary, but for the sensitive sensation seeker, it may be a lifeline and the best way to working with our energies rather than against their natural flow.

Meaningful work

"I dislike superficiality." 91% agreed or strongly agreed with this statement.

With any discussion of work, we must realistically acknowledge our differences. The distribution of people with both traits is likely bell curve shaped with most people somewhere in the vast middle. Some will be at the extreme high end of sensitivity or sensation seeking, or may be higher in one than the other. Obviously, if you are higher in sensation seeking the sensitive side will likely take a beating. If you are higher in sensitivity, the sensation seeking may be dampened. Wherever we may fall along a continuum we all have a deep, human need for meaningful work.

Thrill

Average Person

Low Sensation Seeker

Most People

High Sensation Seeker

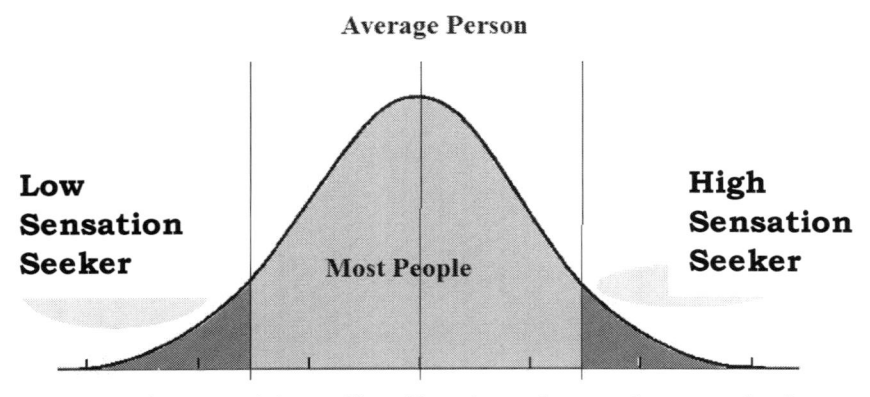

Sensation seeking distribution through population

Meaning in work may be thought of in several dimensions: personal relevance (i.e. I am able to develop my talents and abilities), and relevance to others (i.e. my work positively impacts the lives of others). Personally meaningful work is usually based on increasing complexity that allows for the growth of the individual. Work that does not allow for opportunities for growth and development may set up the conditions in which boredom, anxiety, depression, and a sense of helplessness may take hold and fester.

"I do not need a lot of autonomy in my work." 75% *disagreed or strongly disagreed with this statement.*

Meaningful work allows for *autonomy* on the part of workers. Being free to carry out a task in the best, most efficient way engages our creativity, our energies, and focuses our attention in ways that more structured work cannot. Autonomy is one of the most mentioned desirable attributes for any position in the workplace because it increases self-esteem, productivity, and allows for a sense of personal control. For sensitive sensation seekers, the need for autonomy in how we carry out our work may be irresistible and an ever-present source of tension if not accommodated.[25]

Career opportunities

Sensitive sensation seekers are a very interesting sub-group of the overall highly sensitive population comprising approximately one-third of HSPs with a need for new and novel stimulation (whether in the form of thrill and adventure seeking or experience and novelty seeking) coupled with boredom susceptibility, and disinhibition. Such a group might seem difficult to match to any particular career, but there are situations that work out quite well when our needs as sensitive sensation seekers are met while balancing and respecting both sides. In this section, we will explore potentialities inherent in and expressed by sensitive sensation seekers.

Creatively driven

"As a HSS/HSP, we're always going to be going for the hard stuff because it's almost viscerally painful for us not to go for that new frontier." –Prisha

New Frontiers of Creativity

Exploring a new frontier always requires certain attributes. One of the most useful is creativity. Creativity has suffered a great deal in western society from reductionism which equates all creative activity to producing an end product (artwork, performance, etc.) and is relegated to those who display such abilities (artists and performers). As I suggested in *Thrive* creativity is inherent in all people and is better thought of as finding new and better ways to accomplish a given task or bringing a new concept into being and, in a larger sense, is aimed at creating a life that comprises a "constellation of meaning personally defined."[20]

Thrill

Creativity, in this more inclusive definition, is a drive to solve the problems we encounter in life through constructive efforts to fashion and shape our ever-unfolding realities. Just as a wave breaks against the sand on a beach and dissipates its energy only to return again and again reconstituted in a slightly different form so do each of the chapters of our lives. Creativity is far more than producing an end product or any orientation toward art or performance (though it may be): it is a fundamental drive in all people to seek advantage, to satisfy our exploratory instinct, and to find ways to engage our imaginations in a multitude of ways. For sensitive sensation seekers, this creative drive seems particularly strong.

"My whole business is an act of creation. I've never taken a single business course. It's a highly regarded business, rated by Standard and Poor's. I just started it from instinct. It was a huge act of creation that began with instinct and intuition that was a deep knowing, a fork in the road. I was absolutely right; that was a pivotal point in my life that got me out from under that whole slave mentality of working for someone else." –Danny

"I was practically always on my own and was always creative. I would write and use music as my therapy all of my life. I made my own world of imagination." –Mia

"Being a high sensation seeker we are constantly being asked by our own curious nature to try new things." –Jane

"I've been an artist and found ultimately that it lacked meaning for me. People often praised my work and said how lucky I was, but I felt like being a creative person meant something more. What that was I wasn't sure of, but I had the intuitive, felt instinct that what it meant was

something larger that could include my entire life and not just focus on painting or some other medium." –Matt

"I don't think of creative as always creating physical things. I think of it as creative in your mind. I'm creative about always finding ways to do things. I do create things like jewelry and hats, which I sew, but I'm really creative around the house with fabric and seeing an object and what it could be. People tell me they wish they could be creative like me, but it just comes easy for me." –Hannah

"I think of myself as a creative entrepreneur." –Prisha

Danny is perhaps one of the best exemplars of seamlessly blending creativity with a career. His description of coming to a "fork in the road" where a choice must be made that allows greater personal autonomy, flexibility, and control is something most of us can identify with as we face a more uncertain, less secure workplace environment. Danny instinctively "fell" into self-employment, in his words:

"I stumbled into a tree trimming business because my brothers had been doing it. Within a few weeks, I was making more money than I had been doing plumbing for months. That was 27 years ago, and I'm still doing it today. I wear many hats: I'm the boss, the salesman, I'm a tree climber. I do paperwork; I do the whole thing. It's usually very fulfilling. I have moments where I'm pretty burned out, but it comes and goes in waves. I think of the human dilemma and animals where an animal gets up, and it doesn't know if it's going to make a kill that day and it's exciting for them. I like the excitement of not knowing if I'm going to make $500 or $3,500. It can be straining and stressful, but it's a different kind of stress, not like punching a clock. Sales is exciting. Every customer I meet I never know if they're going to sign or how much I might

make. There's the whole adrenaline thing of climbing trees too."

Self-employment may be a very good fit for some sensitive sensation seekers and provide stimulation that falls within our preferred range of stimulation or the range where we are neither under stimulated or over stimulated. Danny is clearly a thrill and adventure seeker as well as an experience and novelty seeker. The path to self-employment for Danny was a matter of exploring more conventional situations:

"I had trouble holding jobs. I couldn't stand working for people or being under somebody else's control. I always felt like a slave. From 16-23 I was always moving from one job to the next. Then I went in the Job Corps and learned to be a plumber. I did that for three years as well as got married. I had some problems dealing with bosses and at 27-28 I had this real crisis when I took a really hard look at working for other people. I would get up early and just go out running (I wasn't even a runner) and somewhere in all that running and burning off all that energy I decided that I was never going to work for anyone else ever again. I started a plumbing company, but that was really hard because there was too much competition and I had no capital to start with. Then I started a little painting business painting houses, but it didn't fit my temperament because the harder and faster I worked the more mistakes I made and I didn't like that."

Conscientiousness is a trait sensitive people typically have in abundance as we approach any project.[26] Danny's need to do things well, to not make what he considered mistakes was at odds with the fast-paced reality of running a painting business. When he discovered tree trimming he found his niche and was able to blend his needs for conscientious work with his creative nature, while utilizing his empathy and creativity:

"Just knowing how to talk to people and what they want their tree to look like through reading their aesthetic senses and translating that into the work I do."

Self-employment may be one viable avenue to pursue for sensitive sensation seekers, but I recommend doing so only with the greatest of caution and forethought. Self-employment may mean we are in greater overall control of our careers, but we are also ultimately responsible for any and all failures that may occur. Some sensitive sensation seekers may not be well-suited to the vagaries of running a business with all the inherent responsibilities and risks. For others, it might be just the ticket that provides the best compromise between flexibility, creative engagement, and opportunity. There is another aspect that self-employment may offer that is of great potential benefit to creative souls: that is the greater possibility of entering states of flow.

The flow state

"The way to grow while enjoying life is to create a higher form of order out of the entropy that is an inevitable condition of living." Mihaly Csikszentmihalyi

Flow states, or those moments when we are completely engaged in challenging tasks that test our capabilities are not new, now psychologist Mihaly Csikszentmihalyi has studied and applied the idea of flow states to many facets of life. What he has found is that we create our optimal experiences by stretching ourselves to accomplish difficult, challenging tasks. For the self-employed flow states may often occur as new challenges focus our attention on the next difficult (and potentially business ending) crisis.

Thrill

Flow states constitute a range of conditions while engaged in the task: the goals are clear at every step; feedback is immediate; our skills are matched to the task (neither overmatched or under-matched); we find that our attention becomes intensely focused on the task; all other concerns fall away; we lose all self-consciousness and fear of failure; we often lose track of time; and the task becomes autotelic (worth doing for its own sake).[27]

Far from it being true that leisure makes us happy challenging work/tasks truly allow for our growth and development at greater levels of complexity. The entropy Csikszentmihalyi spoke of is likely a byproduct of the anxiety and depression we may experience when we are not engaged in flow states reasonably often. Sensitive sensation seekers may feel a stronger need than others to explore that new frontier, create a new and novel business no one has thought of, or otherwise create niches for ourselves that keep us within our preferred range of arousal. The flow state unites us as sensitives and sensitive sensation seekers. As Prisha stated, *"the boredom was physically painful. If I look back I'm actually surprised I worked at jobs as long as I did. It was so incredibly painful for me that for my own sanity I had to figure something else out."*

"I have problems keeping attention sometimes. I can't just write unknowingly knowing where it's going to go or I lose interest. I'm more likely to put things off if I am not able to get things done. I like having multiple things going on. I need an ending date so I can get it done. It's hard for me to finish projects sometimes." –Claire

"Boredom is definitely an issue for me: a big one. I'm very impatient. I easily get bored. Boredom for me is something that is like hurting you, draining your energy. More recently I'm seeing that it's good to have discipline." –Freja

"When I'm in a flow state, all my other cares instantly cease to be, and I am committed and engaged entirely in the task at hand. Recently I was painting some shutters on my house and thinking how deeply I focus on doing the job really well. The challenge in seeing a rather ordinary task like painting as a challenge to be absolutely present in the moment is a relief from my otherwise overactive mind." – Matt

"Boredom and isolation. I can very easily pick up on that. I catch myself feeling bored and unfulfilled by tuning into my HSP self, in my body and in my actions as I move into lethargy. I choose carefully what I do, but I definitely choose something." – Jacquelyn

If we think of boredom as part of a cycle that is systemic with one cycle influencing the ebb and flow of another, we can think of it as playing a role in our overall development of multipotentiality. Boredom certainly is not a fun state to find oneself in, but it does serve as an incentive to get moving or to make changes. At times boredom may feel defeating and lead to depression or feelings of hopelessness (if the situation is not expected to change or improve). In some careers, in fact, in many jobs, there is always a percentage of tasks that may prove somewhat boring. I acknowledge that reality and do not advocate for unrealistic expectations that we should never tolerate a certain amount of repetitive, boring tasks. Instead, I suggest that when we encounter a boring task that must be done, we do so in a mindful way that is calm, present, and enhances our sense of peace and joy. How do we do this?

Every task will be accomplished one way or another. The choice we have is whether we will go about it grumbling or do so with the full presence of mind. I have encountered my share of boring, repetitive tasks and, at

Thrill

times, have become very adept at "tuning out." Interestingly, Csikszentmihalyi has found that people who frequently engage in the flow experience are more easily able to shut down mental processes unnecessary to the task at hand. *In effect, they are able to control their consciousness.*[28] Boring tasks are also made so much more tolerable if they are shared. It doesn't hurt to have a sense of humor as well. Humor may go a long way in an otherwise depressing situation!

Lifesaver

Self-employment may be a literal life saver for some sensitive sensation seekers allowing us to earn an income simultaneously while experiencing the conditions under which flow states might occur. Most small businesses are fairly specialized and are founded on providing that expertise to the community. When we seek out continual challenge in the form of flow states utilizing our special knowledge we not only aspire to greater levels of proficiency we also enhance our ability to provide that to our customers and communities.

One positive aspect of being a sensitive sensation seeker with great significance in the world is that we may develop into visionary leaders who produce innovative products, services, and re-vision ways of being that carry over into society as it renegotiates itself on a constant basis. One need only observe the extreme wrangling taking place in this election year (2016) where strongly held beliefs often clash on a monumental scale to understand and appreciate that our world desperately needs less extreme, yet innovative and visionary leaders.

Visionary leadership

"My vision for the long term is that we are collectively making a difference in the world and that a group who is

fully realized in themselves, who feel confident and understand themselves and others and are willing to take action in whatever ways they feel compelled to do is going to make a huge difference. I'm a huge Star Trek fan, and I always think about how we can get closer to a larger vision where poverty is eliminated, people get along, and people can live their purpose." –Chloe

"I see us as the agitators and the challengers, the leaders who push the boundaries a bit, albeit in a different way. I think in a slightly different way, and that's why I'm happier being self-employed: I can generate new ideas with ease, but following other people's rules is a bit of a challenge for me." –Robyn

"We open the collective conscious to the unconscious and tap the crown chakra of society. We tap it open to the spiritual dimension. Society could go on with science and mathematics and engineering and function perfectly, but what would be the meaning without journeying to all of the complexities of the soul? Sometimes it takes a bad life event to open us up to our deeper life needs. The breadth and depth of our spiritual journeys open us up to the distance we feel from our culture. Living as an HSS/HSP is a life of extremes between balancing the two for me." – Danny

Chloe, Robyn, and Danny express three differing, yet very promising viewpoints on the role that sensitive sensation seekers may play in our overall society. Chloe's focus is on the collective and helping all people realize their potential through the elimination of barriers that too often stand in the way of people developing the kind of personal confidence and resilience necessary for advancement. Chloe envisions carrying this out through our embodiment of radical awareness of self and others.

Thrill

Robyn subscribes to a free flowing view of leadership where being self-employed allows for the creation of social change through strategic innovation at the cutting edge of society where boundaries may be challenged and redefined. Robyn is the type of creative entrepreneur Prisha spoke of where value-added services and products are developed while allowing for the continual personal refinement of the entrepreneur. In this sense action blends with intent and exciting and transformative processes may take place.

Danny's contribution is the spiritual seeker who journeys within and attempts to make sense of the untoward events of life in a search for meaning. The implications for a society that acts from a center of balance (beginning within) instead of projecting anger, violence, and fear onto others would be dramatic. Spiritual seekers need not represent an organized religious tradition to have an impact on society. Standing independent of organized traditions allows for us to make sense of life without a predetermined structure of meaning.

Leadership for the sensitive sensation seeker may also take more conventional forms where we work within companies and organizations providing our unique brand of energy that is well-suited to creativity, innovation, and moving projects and people forward.

"I'm an INFP. A bunch of us at work did the Myers-Briggs Type Inventory, and it came out as INFJ's and INFP's. It is bizarre to work with so many people that are exactly the same. We can discuss things that I could not discuss anywhere else because we are all HSPs. They love me because I get that HSP part. They love the fact that they are being supported. I think my role is to tell the rest of the world about HSPs and to encourage them, to embrace them

because they are the deep thinkers, they are the artists. We're deeper thinkers, and I think the rest of the world can benefit. That's my job as an HSS; it's my job: to stand up for all the HSPs." –Eleanor

"I think sensation seekers, in general, get very bored from having to sell. They feel they shouldn't have to, that the merits of an idea should stand for itself. Learning that this is where selling and influencing come in and where our personal journeys of self-soothing and working with our sensitivity can help us move other people toward the goal. Not everyone is going to get to our ideal vision where they should be, and that's completely okay." –Prisha

"Our uniqueness is so varied. Because we pick up more data from the environment, we have more to work with. Sometimes that's a good thing, and sometimes it's not so useful depending on where you are. My sensitivity helps me know where to go with the kids, and my sensation seeking helps me communicate flexibly. Some of my colleagues have one communication style. I can adjust to any child's style. The combination of high sensitivity and high sensation is great in that situation." –Nicki

Sensitive sensation seekers may make wonderful leaders if, in Nicki's words, we can learn to be "less caught up in our thinking," and more attuned to a relaxed sense of peace with who and what we are. The more we learn to accept who we are, including our various propensities, the more able we are to *control our consciousness* and *be* in the world in ways that leverage our strengths. This may sound idealistic (controlling our consciousness), yet it's what we do every day when we focus on any task and move outside of our minds. For those in leadership positions tasked with accomplishing a myriad of goals we serve the functional role of process masters, yet we also serve as role models to others (including HSPs). Knowing ourselves and being at peace with ourselves invites others into our experience energizing and reviving others.

Job satisfaction and job choice

The types of jobs we take have a great deal to do with our inherent personality traits, which determine to some degree our preferences and predilections. For the sensitive sensation seeker the ever-present problem of boredom susceptibility combines with an initial period of high interest and adequate stimulation as we learn the various tasks involved in any new job, but then the boredom begins to creep in as we no longer feel challenged by the demands of the position. This may be true for anyone, but for the sensitive sensation seeker who requires new, novel, and varied stimulation, combined with meaningful work that allows a good deal of autonomy many jobs may become stifling and oppressive rather quickly.

Certainly, we all must work to provide for our needs, but we are not mere work animals tasked with only focusing on our daily bread. Finding satisfaction in our careers is an elusive quest for many sensitive sensation seekers.

"One of the things I struggle with is whether I have lived up to my full potential. Career wise I can't keep a job. I become so overstimulated that I can't go to work, I can't show up. I was doing a lot of jobs dealing with many people. If I had worked in a toll booth, I might have been fine. I'm looking at counseling as a possible field because it may provide the intellectual stimulation I'm looking for, but the excitement component I'm going to have to find elsewhere. I used to go out dancing early and leave when it got busy, but I don't really feel safe doing that here so I

haven't found anything that gives me that same kind of outlet. Just to do a job and be drained by it and feel very little satisfaction from it isn't a good fit for me. I did some volunteer work for CASA and really thought that I was moving into something meaningful, but then I realized these people working with the kids have to do what is according to the law, and that really bothered me. I couldn't deal with it because I was a volunteer with no skin in the game and being attacked in court. I felt like the law didn't have any common sense in it. It's important for me to do something meaningful that helps other people." –Jessica

"I decided I wanted to be a landscape designer, and I went out and took classes and did some pro bono work. I developed this small portfolio and decided to move somewhere where the growing season was a lot longer. I moved 900 miles away. I just up and did it after months of contemplation. Sometimes I really struggle with corporate think: lack of long term planning or busy work and it's a real struggle to be who I am in that environment, and that's why I think I'm not going to be there forever. I think HSPs can't stay in that; you can't survive for long before you feel like you're losing your soul and you have to find a place that supports you." –Chloe

"I've stayed in this toxic job because I don't want to have to go work with new people. I went on an interview last week and as soon as I walked in all I could smell was desperation. I'm like kill me now! I don't want anything to do with this. I perform at my best when completely alone. I'm not a team player. I perform best when I am completely excited about something…it's just me I can totally get into it and love it. I also function much better at night. The dark and quiet." –Eleanor

"Now, I do wire wrapped jewelry, and I sell t-shirts of my design. This supplements my small pension and allows me

Thrill

to do my own thing in my own way. No status quo or business as usual. Lack of recognition for my accomplishments has led me to leave many jobs. I left my career at 48 to go out and do the things that I wanted to accomplish in life while I was still physically able to, though I was giving up the "security" of the American dream. That took a year in building the courage to take the step. NO REGRETS!" –John

"I've had a series of income producing activities. I would not call it a career until recently. I graduated in 2001, and my goal was to do graduate school and get a masters in industrial organizational psychology. I couldn't afford to move though so I took their offer to defer enrollment and worked as an administrative assistant. I didn't really care for it, but each day was different, and I was really good at it. Each day I talked to different people, and I was good at adapting to the needs of the job. Before that, I waited tables in a restaurant. That was very stressful at first, but I got the hang of it and liked it because it was different every day. I was also able to taste the different specials the kitchen put out each week. I did that in their different restaurants for about three months each. I got a little bored in each one and realized there was nowhere to move up, and that's why I needed to find a new job." –Jane

Job satisfaction has much to do with job choice and, as we have seen from the quotes above, sometimes we choose jobs out of necessity or convenience without due regard for the long-term. Each job may provide one or more aspects that we value (meaningfulness, autonomy, variety), but may ultimately leave us wanting more. Feeling like we have lived up to our full potential seems to be a major issue for many sensitive sensation seekers as we continue our lonely, frustrating quests for job satisfaction that seems to be over and above what others (those without the traits) experience.

Recommendations

While I cannot offer highly specific advice about what careers might work best for sensitive sensation seekers due to the deeply individualized nature of each of our lives (some are more sensation seeking, others are more sensitive, with personal choices/preferences playing major roles) I can offer some general guidelines that should prove informative based on the research:

- For those high in boredom susceptibility employment situations where short-term projects and job responsibilities with flexibility built-in may work well (in fact may be essential for you). This may be with an employer or as a self-employed person. Depending on how high you may be in either trait (or specific aspects of each trait) will ultimately determine the best fit for you. Explore and try new positions or combinations of things that each generate income streams and provide stimulation. Drop things that fail to work or quit working and think of your various endeavors as constantly evolving to meet your needs. *Ride that wave of flexibility.*
- Self-employment may be a very good option for sensitive sensation seekers for whom autonomy and flexibility are paramount. Being self-employed is certainly no guarantee of financial or career success (and it does carry with it all the numerous responsibilities of running a business), but for some, it may be just the ticket. Pay attention to the cautious, careful part of yourself that demands you thoroughly research, reflect, and evaluate your options for opening a business, but then don't be afraid to go for it!

Thrill

- If you find that you are more impulsive, consider contract assignments if possible where you may have time between assignments to pursue your thrill and adventure seeking or to seek novelty and new experiences. Not all people will fit one mold. Some will need to live the life of the bohemian traveling the country in a renovated VW bus or live on a houseboat part of the year and in a treehouse the rest. Who knows? Your niche might be that you have no niche, yet I am sure you are quite knowledgeable and capable in the right circumstances. That does not affect your ability to experience a full life nor do you need to justify your existence to anyone else. *Your value is in who you are and how you treat others.*
- If you are higher in sensitivity, it's likely you prefer a quieter environment where you are more able to control your physical and interpersonal environment, so you have time and space to think deeply and regulate your emotional energy. Though you may think of this as a hassle (having to manage for overstimulation) you are probably an excellent planner and have considered all possible angles and pick up on subtle cues others miss. You are also probably very empathic and can read the emotional states of others quite easily. Such an individual, combined with the extra boost of being a sensation seeker, may make an excellent leader, teacher, healthcare provider, or entrepreneur (just to name a few possible choices). Your real challenge as a sensitive sensation seeker will be to establish and maintain a balance between your competing needs for novelty and new stimulation without overwhelming the quieter, more reflective part.

Trade Work

Sensitive sensation seekers work in every possible field, but many are concentrated in the "helping" professions. It's easy to see how being able to work directly with people in capacities like healthcare and education may provide both the stimulation we need as sensation seekers along with the meaningful part so valued by our sensitive selves. Beyond that though there is another realm of work that is too often overlooked as we discuss careers and that is the trades. Jobs that require only trade/vocational school education, plus some on the job experience may not only pay as well (sometimes better) than professional work requiring advanced college degrees and too often quite a lot of financial debt that can hamper future well-being and long-term planning, but also provide flow experiences on a regular basis.

We sensitive sensation seekers are made for flow experiences because of our boredom susceptibility and novelty seeking which makes us well suited to relatively short-term projects. Flow experiences challenge us while providing opportunities for mastery and growth. Trade work often involves some degree of physical labor, which makes it different than professional work in that it engages our whole bodies in focusing on the task at hand. That level of engagement can be all-consuming in ways that are actually therapeutic for some. There are other advantages too in the form of often increased autonomy over professional work, greater connection to tangible results (a working car that was formerly broken, a roof repaired that leaked, a hairstyle that enhances another person's appearance and self-confidence, or a mended water pipe), and often greater acceptance of individual differences. In professional settings people are often judged by how they appear and act with great pressure to conform to the "company way." In trade work outsiders are usually the norm and few people care about your appearance or behaviors as long as you are able to do your work well and are dependable.

Trade work may require some specialized training, but often one can begin as a journeyman or apprentice and work up to higher levels of competence and responsibility. It's entirely possible to build a very good business on a low-key idea like cleaning offices, for example, or yard care. There are a thousand ways to get into a trade or start a small business utilizing simple, easily acquired skills with the potential to make a decent living and preclude involvement with the often predatory corporate world.

Similarly, sensitive sensation seekers may do better than one might think in military service. Military service provides a broad range of possible occupational specialties that are directly applicable to civilian life. You might think "The military? Are you kidding?" The truth is military service has changed a great deal, even from my time in the military during the 1980s. Today's military is more integrated, more inclusive, and knows they are dealing with a different group of recruits with different needs than 30 years ago. Most people think of the military as perpetual boot camp with drill sergeants constantly yelling and threatening. What a life for a sensitive sensation seeker right? The reality is once basic training is finished recruits move on to advanced occupational training then to permanent units where they perform their jobs (no drill sergeants). Often these jobs may be real-world appropriate and transferable. My advice? Don't completely discount the military because it may offer very valuable training, plus quite a bit of money for college if military service is completed along with other very worthwhile benefits.

There are numerous ways we can experience flow, but with regards to career we should look at fields that offer us the best possible compromise between flow experiences and overall conditions. We don't necessarily need to land that "ultimate" job, but we do need to find work that will work for us! Each of us will have realities we will have to face like educational attainment (many people are just not cut out for college), geographic limitations (what's available in the area you live), and familial considerations (who counts on us and does that mean more than moving a thousand miles away for a great job). As we age we may also face health limitations. Cumulative stress takes a physical and emotional toll on people, but especially sensitive sensation seekers who must constantly manage for overstimulation, negative stimulation, and working environments with manipulative, exploitive, arrogant, or unpleasant people. There is a *huge* burnout factor for sensitives and sensitive sensation seekers we must factor in as we discuss the overall picture of career.

Ideally we are able to find a workable career field, adapt to it in time, and have our needs met, but too often with sensitives and sensitive sensation seekers our needs are not met and we face either putting our heads down and simply grumbling along or leaving the position in an often perpetual merry-go-round of jobs forever in search of "something" that will work well enough. The instability and interruptions in income have real effects on our families and on our self-esteem. This is especially true in societies that heavily equate self-worth with what we do (our occupation).

Questions and Answers

I've job hopped a lot in my life and feel like I may never find one great job that makes me happy.

Sensitive sensation seekers may indeed experience more trouble with finding a singular career that fits them well. I suggest rather than thinking in terms of one career satisfying all of our needs for novelty, new stimulation, meaningfulness, autonomy, etc. that we think more in terms of crafting lives where we create multiple income streams from several sources with built-in flexibility allowing us to ebb and flow with what works best at the moment. In that sense we are always engaged in activities that stimulate us well and that are productive. It may also be that we need to look beyond career to provide life satisfaction. Career certainly consumes much of our waking time, but we should not discount the role of the socialization we choose and that may, in fact, prove to be more satisfying. Life is not a singular event or process, it is a series of interconnected systems and processes that feed our needs on multiple fronts. We should embrace that complexity and detach ourselves from limiting cultural notions of one career or of our happiness as being tied to following a predictable life path. You *may* find a career that works very well for you, but it's likely that you will change careers several times during your working lifetime and move from position to position within those careers.

I have always wanted to be self-employed, but I am afraid of the whole thing.

It's natural to fear the unknown, but as with most things as you begin to research you will likely find that the more you know, the less you fear. There are many great resources available online that can help you develop greater confidence in constructing your business idea. Don't be afraid to enlist the help of knowledgeable others (those who have or are already in business) to help you with planning and execution. Running a business is not a sprint, it's more of a marathon where patience is punctuated by bold action, where maintaining a moderate pace is better than exhausting our energies all at once, and where we may find a great deal of satisfaction on many fronts. I suggest easing into a business if possible by continuing your present job. Never assume your great business idea will translate into profit in the short-term or that you will be able to rely on consistent profits for some time. As you grow and learn the business you are in you will gradually gain more confidence personally and professionally. Joining a small business support group (either locally or online) may be a great way to find support as you go through the startup and growth process.

Key Takeaways

- Empathy is one of the hallmarks of sensitivity and may be utilized as an effective way of relating to and managing the behavior of others. Empathy is a great advantage, but must be carefully managed for overstimulation.
- Boredom susceptibility is a major issue for most sensitive sensation seekers. Engaging in flow states often may help us stay ahead of boredom.
- Self-employment may be a lifesaver for sensitive sensation seekers who find themselves incompatible with conventional employment situations. One should seek to diversify income streams for maximum flexibility and security against downturns.
- The sensitive sensation seeker may be a visionary leader with tremendous implications for non-dualistic, altruistic action in the world. Boredom susceptibility, however, is an ever-present problem. Thus we are best suited to short-term projects with definite ending dates.

Thrill

- Sensitive sensation seekers have a creative drive that may be harnessed to create lives where creativity permeates every level.
- The flow experience is especially good for sensitive sensation seekers because of our boredom susceptibility and the need for short-term projects offering fresh challenges with growth opportunities and greater complexity.
- Trade work may be a very viable option for some sensitive sensation seekers because it may offer greater autonomy, more personal acceptance, is easily entered into, and entrepreneurship may enable the creation of a profitable business.
- Military service may be an option worth considering because one can be vocationally trained (for free), have strong structure (if that is a desirable element), and possibly experience some great duty assignments with long-term benefits like education, healthcare, and a home loan. Care must be taken however in ensuring good choices are made in vocational choice.

Chapter 4
Relationships

"Nothing is perfect. Life is messy. Relationships are complex. Outcomes are uncertain. People are irrational." – Hugh Mackay

The imperfect, messy, complex, uncertain, irrational nature of relationships may make anyone wonder why we spend so much time and effort on developing and maintaining good relationships and why we suffer in bad relationships so long. For sensitive sensation seekers, relationships are complicated by our concurrent need for stimulation within an optimum range, boredom susceptibility, and need to find a partner who can simultaneously identify and be compatible with our often contradictory natures. Finding a partner with the ability or potential to relate to us in such a way as to support and encourage our development, while doing the same in their lives may be quite a difficult task. In this crucial chapter, we cover the major aspects of relationships in the lives of sensitive sensation seekers.

Types of love

We all have many types of interpersonal relationships in our lives: work relationships (consisting of superiors, subordinates, and peers), friend relationships that range from quite casual to more intimate, and close love relationships with family and significant others. In addition to the messy nature of conducting these relationships, we also juggle, in many cases, some form of love for others. Love relationships can seem immensely complex so let's talk about types of love first before we move on.

Thrill

C.S. Lewis wrote that there are four main types of love: storge (pronounced store-gay), philia (fill-ee-ah), eros (air-os), and agape (a-gah-pay).[29] *Storge* (from the Greek) is the sort of love shared between children and parents, friends and colleagues, even pets and owners. As the least picky type of love, we may develop affection for anyone without any form of attraction. Storge has been characterized as empathy bonding where we come to feel affection for another person through familiarity.

Philia may be thought of as the type of bond that exists between *real* friends. True friendship is rare these days, but it may be as strong as the bond between siblings and last as long. Philia is freely given to choice people in our lives (if you have been so lucky as to find worthy people to give it to) and it grows out of companionship. A good example of philia and how it differs from storge is at work. Most of us have developed casual friendships at work and seen many others do the same, but occasionally we experience a friendship that goes beyond mere familiarity into true friendship. Philia is a deeply appreciative love few of us experience in our modern rushed, superficial world, but may also be one of the most satisfying.

Eros is more familiar to most of us as erotic love, which includes sexual love. Eros goes beyond a desire for sexual intimacy with another person and focuses instead on the desire to *be* with someone. For anyone who has ever fallen in love this feeling is familiar as our thoughts are maddeningly preoccupied with the object of our affection. The experience of Eros may be one of the most powerful of our lives. Lastly, *Agape* represents unconditional, altruistic love we exercise on other people's behalves. Our feelings are not necessarily involved in agape. Thus attraction to the person is not involved.[29]

Canadian psychologist John Alan Lee describes several other types of love that exist beyond Lewis' conceptualization including *ludus* (loo-dus), *pragma* (prag-muh), and *philautia* (phil-aw-teeuh). *Ludus* is playful, no strings attached, uncommitted love. *Pragma* is shared love for the sake of long-term mutual benefit. *Philautia* is self-love, taken to an extreme may be narcissism, but in a milder form may be the basis for all love directed toward others (loving yourself first enables you to love others).[30]

Together the types of love we have identified permeate our various relationships to one degree or another with some love types overlapping or giving way (evolving in time) from one to another (as in eros to agape, as one possible example). Researchers typically have looked at the psychological facets of human love, but there are very likely genetic aspects as well including the dopaminergic and serotonergic pathways in our brains. That is to say; our love behaviors are affected and influenced partly by our psychology and our genetics. To simplify this down to something more manageable let's lay out two broad categories: passionate love and companionate love.

Passionate versus companionate love

Passionate love we are all familiar with as a deep longing for union with our beloved that preoccupies our emotions and time. We may feel intense emotions of anxiety at their loss or elation in their presence. We are less emotionally stable, prone to jealousy at the mere hint of infidelity or loss of affection. Passionate love, in short, affects the way we think, feel, and act while involved with the object of our affections. For this reason, *passionate love is not easy to maintain, nor is it necessarily desirable to do so due to its impairing effects*. In fact, passionate love was not even a precondition to marriage until twelfth century Europe when notions of undying, unconditional love became popular. Prior to that time, passionate love was not connected to marriage.[31] We might find that to be quite amazing today considering that most people choose to base their marriage choices on passionate love.

Companionate love, on the other hand, relies less on intense emotion and more on a deep sense of caring and commitment to another person. Companionate love may still contain strong emotional bonds, but the sense of needing to possess the partner is lessened, as is jealousy, sexual frequency, and emotional instability. Companionate love is suitable for a lifetime, while passionate love, due to its unstable nature, is less sustainable.[31]

Attachment styles

There is another fundamental aspect of human bonding we must define before moving on to a larger discussion of relationships and sensitive sensation seekers. Attachment style comes to us from our early associations with others (mother, father, caregivers, etc.). Based on how well we could expect others to respond to our needs we may develop a secure, avoidant, or anxious/ambivalent attachment style.[32]

In a *secure* style, we know our needs will be met, and we venture forth with a minimum of anxiety and fear knowing others "have our back" so to speak. In an *avoidant* style, we attempt to keep our distance in a relationship preferring self-reliance over intimacy. In an avoidant style we have learned that people are not to be trusted. Therefore we keep them at arm's length and withhold our affections. In an *anxious/ambivalent* style, we artificially try to maintain closeness for fear our partner will abandon us. The anxiety of potential loss creates a feeling of needing to merge completely with the person to avoid their loss, which we are sure will happen.

The type of attachment style we have developed carries over into our adult lives deeply impacting the way we conduct our relationships. I am an advocate of raising our consciousness so that we are self-aware of our tendencies and do not act blindly and unknowingly damaging and destroying the relationships in our lives. The more we know and are aware of these tendencies the better we should be able to make choices that are appropriate for ourselves and others. In some cases that may mean we know we are anxious/ambivalent and need to work on our fear of loss and abandonment. If we know we are avoidant, we know we are pushing people away rather than allowing ourselves to experience real intimacy. If we are secure in our attachment style, we know we are likely to trust others to meet our needs and that we are more comfortable meeting the needs of others. In all cases, self-knowledge is empowering, though what we do with that knowledge is up to each of us.

Close love relationships

There are many types of relationships we might have throughout our lives, but none provide the intensity of emotions and depth of feeling as our close love relationships. The significant others in our lives can make or break our chances of success and happiness as too many of us discover after suffering in poor relationships for too long. I was particularly interested in the types of partners that sensitive sensation seekers chose and what their experiences were like as I sought to explore this crucial bedrock area of life.

"I was married for 17 years to a sociopath. He was very controlling and would get crazy if I were like gone to the

Thrill

store too long. He would accuse me of cheating on him. I woke up in my 40s and just thought "Who have I been?" At first there were feelings of guilt and being confused because I'm very honest and take care of everyone." –Carla

"I dated a few men before I got married at 23. I never learned what respect or setting boundaries looked like, so the marriage wasn't built on respecting boundaries. Being a people pleaser is all I knew. Everyone else was more important than me and it came natural for me to put the needs of others before mine, including and especially my ex. He is a college educated engineer. Graduated in the top 5% of his class. He had a job before graduating. We got married the same year he graduated college. During our 25 year marriage, we traveled and I became a stay at home mom. He became more controlling and absent during those years. That's when we became strangers. We divorced in 2004." –Christine

"Growing up my Mom was very dramatic and with my boyfriend I've wanted to have drama because I equated it with love. I couldn't figure out that I could still love someone without feeling intense emotions all the time. We've gotten through that part where too many emotions were too much. I much prefer this comfortable stage. It's less intense feelings, less drama. The sensation seeking was hard because it did some damage in the beginning. I grew a lot and learned from it. My boyfriend has calmed me down." –Claire

"I was watching television once and there was this girl that I felt this connection with, just this powerful magnetic pull. Out of the blue some people showed up for a movie and I went over to the movie set and started talking to this very beautiful girl and she turned out to be this girl from the tv show! They were just there for the set, which was apparently hard to find. I became really close to this girl *and it was a high point in my life. She ended up leaving with the crew before I could say goodbye. That was the beginning of my deep, interior journey, a deep spiraling into darkness that lasted several years. That strange sense of cosmic connection sent me onto this deep search brought on by this bad experience. Now I understand that she was a kindred spirit, but that took a long time. I've come to see over time and studying that it's very important to be with kindred spirits."* –Danny

"I have chosen to stay alone. There's lots of creepy people around so I decided to take care of my daughters on my own. I've been married twice. I'm apparently not very good at picking." –Eleanor

"Finding men who don't think I'm just being difficult because I need certain things to be comfortable is hard. I feel like they just don't get me and I know I can be very intuitive and know right away when meeting someone how comfortable I will be with them. I used to just go along with whatever the guy wanted to do because growing up I really never felt like my thoughts or feelings were valid. I was afraid to speak up for myself. Going along with things was easier. Now I don't care anymore and if someone wants to be with me they can make the effort. I feel like I'm only compatible with like one half percent of men out there." – Hannah

"In my serious relationships my sensation seeking was endearing, but, in the long run I was too insecure for my partners. I have been too accepting, too much of a people pleaser instead of being steadfast in who I am. Never again!" –John

"My partner is also a HSP and an HSS however both of our sensitivities and sensation seeking behaviors show up in different ways. I, for my part, have learned to admit that

recuperating at home is not his preferred way to feed his HSP side as his HSS side gets bored. He would rather go engage in an activity that keeps him active and focused for hours at a time. He, for his part, has had to accept that when we travel or have a busy day I need down time (my HSP side) and when we go meet people I need to be the loud boisterous entertaining story teller (how my extroversion and HSS shows up). Net net we have worked in more time apart in our relationship so we can feed our HSS and HSP in ways that work for both of us." –Prisha

"I was married the first time at 21 to a woman who was not highly sensitive or a sensation seeker. I was the emotional one in that relationship with my strong emotions appearing at times when things were edging toward crisis. I was always amazed how the impending serious issues didn't seem to affect her the same way. I never thought I was overreacting, but I did find myself feeling incredibly frustrated at what seemed like the high threshold for engaging and expressing emotion. Now, I'm married to another sensitive sensation seeker like myself which is actually exponentially more difficult and volatile in some ways due to two emotionally charged people trying to be together." -Matt

"In my first marriage I was with a guy who was very dangerous and I liked it because I was a high sensation seeker. I liked that he showed me new things. With him I started experimenting with different drugs and sexually. I loved it because it was all new. We were together for two years and I shut down. I didn't want to try anything new. I just wanted to get back to normal. It was as if I had pushed my own sensation seeking past my own comfort zone." –Jane

"It used to be difficult to find people who could understand one person could be both: they wanted one or the other. But

my husband of 7 ½ years (he's probably an HSP) loves it all. I think it might have helped for me to accept myself before I met him." –Nicki

Choices, choices so many choices

It's clear from these interviews that we all choose partners based on very different criteria. Some are very careful in vetting and choosing partners, while others seem to be attracted to people who are very much like them (not always to their benefit). Others choose people who are probably not good partner material for the long term and for whom we often spend far too much of our precious lives. The partners we choose have much to do with *propinquity* or the notion that those closest to us in proximity form our most likely pool of candidates. That has, of course, changed a great deal with the advent of online dating, but propinquity is still a major factor in mate choice.

For sensitive sensation seekers the choices may be even more complex as we juggle our need for new and novel sensation (and what may be more stimulating than a new partner?) while searching for someone with whom we can have those deep conversations, express our inner feelings without judgement or fear of ridicule, and embody our sensitivity in a confident way. The sensitive self needs to be heard, held, nurtured, and supported. How can we expect to navigate these complex waters when many of us don't have a good understanding of who we are? Being in a relationship will not complete you as a person if you are suffering from past hardships or lingering resentments. Before we can expect someone else to feel that we are worthy of their love we have to be complete on our own. Not only are confident people more attractive as partners they are also less likely to find themselves in relationships they should have avoided. Make no mistake: the dating

Thrill

world is full of frogs and few princes (and vice versa). When we enter a relationship at less than our best we place ourselves at a disadvantage that may cost us (and others) dearly.

The wild side

For those who are high in thrill and adventure-seeking and/or disinhibition and boredom susceptibility, the bounds of reality may find themselves being stretched a good deal as we let the wild child loose to play. Thrill and adventure seekers love the rush of physical thrills. They love the sense of exhilaration at jumping out of an airplane and plunging thousands of feet through the air only to pull the ripcord and swing to and fro beneath a billowy parachute carrying them safely to the ground. Others may prefer roller coasters, motorcycle riding, rock climbing, or any of a thousand thrill-seeking sports or adventures. Going back to sensation seeking as an evolutionary adaptation those who were high in thrill and adventure-seeking would have probably made good explorer material heading off into unknown areas in search of resources and suitable land. In a relationship thrill and adventure seeking may take other interesting forms such as for Jessica:

"My husband and I were pretty out there and would go to nudist camps and swingers clubs and, while we weren't swingers, we had a friend and we would fool around and looking back I kind of think the sensation seeking was part of it; getting that same kick as in stripping. We haven't done anything like that in about six years. I think it stopped providing the thrill it once did."

Jessica further added that when her wild child was let out *"in that space, I'm completely disinhibited. There're no boundaries there. We went to New Mexico to see these Earthships being built and ended up on the side of a mountain in these natural hot springs with young people smoking pot and running naked through the desert. Weird things happen when I go places. I'll just go off the beaten trail and try anything once. That does make life complicated. Luckily my partner is not controlling or judgmental. My first husband was very controlling and wanted me to be this well-behaved, moneyed ladylike wife: that just wasn't me."*

Carla articulated a similar stance regarding her wild side: "*I had a lot of boyfriends. I went out with a lot of guys. I didn't date any of them for very long before I was done with that flavor. That was when I was younger. For women when you're in your 20s and 30s we're more inhibited, more content to just raise the babies or whatever, but as soon as you hit the 40s you're like "Okay, I'm ready to go crazy!"*

Sensation seeking can be a strong force that overrides our sensitivity, or at least makes it take a back seat at times. This can be useful. Jessica again related "*I was a real daredevil and people could not understand how I could be so withdrawn and do such crazy things. I was a huge rollercoaster junkie and we used to make these tree swings and swing out over 20-30 foot ravines. I dirt bike rode, I climbed trees; I was really a big paradox. I spent a lot of my life trying to push through fear. I couldn't understand how I could feel so overwhelmed in crowds doing things I liked to do like concerts, going to restaurants, and yet those things caused me fear. I like to socialize, yet it leaves me feeling drained like I need to hide in a closet for two days. I couldn't figure out what was going on.*"

Matt related how giving in to the desire or need to have a new experience can be "freeing" as we step outside our comfort zone and discover our limitations may be "further out than we thought they were." Matt's wild side is rooted in an openness to new experiences acknowledging that "we only live this life once, and there's so much to see and do!" In as much as sensitivity and sensation seeking are adaptations that enabled our survival and reproductive success they are also wonderful traits that encourage us to experience life in its fullest realization. Sensation seeking is forever pushing us forward (with boredom as the stick), while sensitivity allows us to slow down and appreciate our experiences. Letting the wild side out to play may also help us break down some of the complexes and phobias we may have developed.

Pushing through fear and disinhibition

Utilizing sensation seeking to help us "push through fear" may be a real positive and represents one of the distinguishable differences in sensitive sensation seekers from sensitives. The extra push to seek out novelty and new experiences combined with disinhibition and boredom susceptibility may be powerful motivators to confront the experiences that scare us thereby opening us up to a broader range of possible behaviors and lived experiences. Another aspect of sensation seeking may help us conquer fear: disinhibition.

Disinhibition is when we push beyond our normal range of behaviors somewhat impulsively in pursuit of the next intense experience. Zuckerman defines disinhibition as "seeking sensation through other people, a hedonistic lifestyle, "wild" parties, sexual variety, and drinking to disinhibit. It is an ancient form of sensation seeking, finding social acceptance in bacchanals and carnivals; shows few if any relationships to education, race, or class."[7]

Certainly, this represents an extreme and most of us have been disinhibited in our lives at one point or another (whether we will admit it or not), but not necessarily to the extreme of what could be considered "wild parties" or having a hedonistic lifestyle. For instance many people like to ride roller coasters, many do not. Sometimes, however, we feel like we want to throw caution to the wind and do something scary (even if it terrifies us). That's a bit less extreme than a hedonistic lifestyle, and one many of us can relate to. Being disinhibited or uninhibited in a relationship allows us to grow as individuals and as couples through shared, intense experiences. Few of us recall the boring experiences, but we do recall that rollercoaster ride!

Disinhibition in relationships may be a powerful force propelling a sensitive sensation seeker toward a new experience. A partner may or may not enjoy this aspect of our personality (depending on the context), but disinhibition may also contribute to keeping the spark of romance and vitality alive in long-term relationships. Pushed to an extreme though disinhibition may override boundaries of respect for our partner and put our relationship at risk. Indulged moderately disinhibition can help individuals and couples to push through fears of new experiences and foster a greater openness in a relationship that can be quite healthy in the long term.

Sexuality

"Males do not represent two discrete populations; heterosexual and lesbian or gay. The world is not to be divided into sheep and goats, and not all things are black nor all things white. It is a fundamental of taxonomy that nature rarely deals with discrete categories. Only the human mind invents categories and tries to force facts into separated pigeon-holes. The living world is a continuum in

each and every one of its aspects. The sooner we learn this concerning human sexual behavior, the sooner we shall reach a sound understanding of the realities of sex." – Alfred C. Kinsey, Sexual Behavior in the Human Male

I have written about the broader range of possible behaviors on the part of HSPs before and advocated that we embody complexity. Rarely do HSPs see issues in terms of pure black and white simplicity because we take in more information and process it more elaborately in the brain and body. Most things, as Kinsey states, are on a continuum with most of us somewhere in the vast middle. There will always be those at the extremes of both ends (high or low sensation seeking or high and low sensitivity), but all of us will experience sexuality throughout our lifetimes. Let's take a look at this often ignored area of relationships and learn what sensitive sensation seekers have to say about their experiences.

"I've most definitely been impulsive with sexual partners in the past. I was confused about the difference between love and sex. The only relationship I had with my ex was a sexual relationship. Seems he thought that's all I had to offer and never really cared to know me on any other level. Even when I became a mother. He never seemed to value the sacrifice I made to stay home with our children. I understand now that he is not capable of seeing value in anyone unless they have the potential to generate significant money. When money became more important to him than anything else, he changed. He was no longer the person I married. He still needed ME to be the social butterfly in the relationship. The person who would talk to his friends and family because he had nothing to say to them. We both changed and counseling didn't help us. At one point in our marriage, I told him, I'm not fulfilled in the marriage. His reply: "I'm totally fulfilled, so if you're not, that's YOUR problem." Through counseling, I learned he

was truly blind to his participation in the deterioration in our marriage. He was totally fulfilled. The problem was me." –Christine

"Definitely way more intense. Light stimulation goes a long way. Awareness of the other person's energy and closeness to it in experience makes sex very colorful and intense for me. Emotional disagreements generally reduce my sex drive more drastically than non-HSPs." –Prisha

"My intensity as an HSP is a core theme throughout my life including all aspects of sex. I appreciate and seek intensity, and good sex must have an intensity about it. There are some challenges around this including in long-term relationships, but these are minimal for me as I have enough natural intensity and understand my own needs. I also seek out partners who are similar to me in relation to this intensity and are more likely to be HSP (at least moderately) so." –Robyn

"Sex is usually fairly intense for me from a purely sensory viewpoint, but while I'm experiencing this intensity and trying to enjoy and enhance the experience I care about the quality of the experience for my partner. I want to know that I am pleasing her and not just myself. It's important to me that there's an emotional connection based on trust." – Matt

"The first ten years after high school I was curious and adventurous and fearless. When I was young, I really enjoyed getting inside other people's "shoes" for a short time, and many of those "adventures" became friendships. I tried a few unusual things. I've always been hetero, but can imagine accepting more fluid situations." –Nicki

It's the intensity, the rush

Thrill

The high sensation seeker is always after the intensity of the experience or the adrenaline rush. Sensation seeking works through the dopaminergic system in our brain whereby the neurotransmitter dopamine is released early in the experience wetting our appetites for more.[7] When we are anticipating hedonic experiences, we often minimize the risks and focus on the benefits (our pleasure). That's part of what makes sex so exciting and more so when the potential sexual partner is new to us. It's the same as in thrill and adventure-seeking: we want the rush of having the experience.

For the sensitive sensation seeker, there is more; the sensitive side may value something more meaningful, less rushed, and less intense because the underlying trait in HSPs (sensory processing sensitivity) works by activating the behavioral inhibition system (BIS). This system prefers reflection over action and sensitivity to subtleties. In contrast to a "rush," the HSP might be more of a patient lover who is in no hurry to arrive at a finish line.

The sensitive sensation seeking lover?

The intensity of experience is a hallmark of sensation seeking. We seek it out in sex, sports, recreation, and in our careers. Sensation seekers (especially those at the high end) may find themselves so painfully bored with repetition as to find it to be not worth doing. Sex may seem like an area of life where boredom would not be a factor, yet it is for most people.

Is this need for new and novel experiences completely incompatible with sensitivity? Can one be a sensitive sensation seeking lover? Remember that sensitivity is also about openness to new experiences and creativity. *In effect, HSPs are hard-wired for creativity, and*

Relationships

that can extend to sexuality. Sensation seekers can feed that creativity with their "devil may care" attitude at times that seeks the rush of doing something new and perhaps naughty. Jessica mentioned how when she's feeling disinhibited she may "go off the beaten trail and try anything once." With sexuality that attitude may be very good for variety's sake, but as Jessica observed these experiences may stop providing the same kick or thrill (in time) as they once did. That's where the sensitive lover may kick in and provide deep companionship, connection, and emotional authenticity.

Christine observed *"I was recently with a group of mature adults who invited me into a hot tub naked. They were naked and invited me to join them. None of their coaxings could get me into a hot tub...period! Would I do it in a secure, monogamous relationship...ABSOLUTELY! One on one with a man who has shown me he cares as much about my soul as he does my body...ABSOLUTELY!! I don't think I've had more sexual partners than others, but I've had a lot of first dates. I guess they can tell; it's going to require more from them, and they aren't interested. I feel I intimidate men. I'm not easy or naïve."*

Christine emphasized the need to view sex as connected and dependent on the health of the overall relationship: *"In my opinion, a physical relationship changes for men and women as we age. It's not going to be like it was in our youth no matter how many blue pills you take. Men tend to have an issue with this. They still define themselves on how well they're able to perform or please a woman in the bedroom. What they don't understand is, how well we connect outside the bedroom has more to do with how well the physical relationship is or will be. I told my ex this years ago, and he didn't get it. Most men don't understand this."*

Thrill

The sensitive sensation seeking lover may, in fact, be the best of both worlds with the excitement of new sexual experiences combined with the comforting security that comes with emotional authenticity in the relationship. This may vary a great deal from person to person depending on how high or low they may be in either trait and on a person's circumstances in life. The better our lives are in general the more at ease we may feel about expressing our sensitive sensation seeking selves as patient, yet potentially exciting lovers and partners. The worse our lives are the less likely it may be that we are able to be fully present in our close love relationships. Being a sensitive sensation seeker in a relationship is similar to other areas of life; imbued with complexity yet loaded with potential joy, happiness, and growth.

Questions and Answers

I'm young and, frankly, kind of wild, but I'm also sensitive and hate superficiality. Will I always be this way? Will I ever find love?

Sensation seeking tends to decline somewhat with age, except for the boredom susceptibility which remains consistent. Sensitivity tends to increase with age, but may be managed with appropriate self-care and awareness. Finding love implies a desire for a long-term relationship with a compatible partner. As we've discussed in this chapter, there are many forms of love. Thus if you're stuck on the idea of passionate, romantic love (as is promoted in western society and is a relatively new idea historically) you may be more apt to go from relationship to relationship when each one fizzles out. Long term relationships need to evolve from passionate love to companionate love. They can coexist and do for many couples, but understand that a long-term relationship needs to be more of a slow simmer than a fast boil.

How can I prevent myself from falling too fast and too hard for a partner?

Experience may be the best teacher here. As sensation seekers, we gravitate to the new and novel and what's more novel than an exciting new person who stirs our emotions? Self-awareness comes with time and should serve to remind us of our predispositions. If we know we are prone to falling too hard and too fast we can consciously choose to slow down and allow something besides our emotions to rule the day.

Would I be compatible with another sensitive sensation seeker?

It's impossible to predict compatibility, but it is more likely, if you desire a long-term relationship, that someone who is similar to you will be better material than someone who is your opposite. Sometimes it may be tempting to think how great it might be to be with another sensitive sensation seeker, but that would truly depend on how both traits are expressed in that person. For instance, how high or low the person is in either trait would be key to their possible behaviors. We might find that another sensitive person would be too much of a trigger for us because of their triggers. It's also possible we could learn from each other and be able to accommodate each other's needs without compromising our own. As we've discussed in this chapter the longer lasting forms of love (companionate love) are better for long-term sustainability than the passionate forms. Who we may find that love with and what traits they may have will likely be similar to our own, but entail a learning curve that may or may not be too steep a price to pay.

What are the best ways to create boundaries in relationships?

Boundaries are lines of trust between partners. When we communicate our needs openly and honestly, a loving partner should respect our needs and accommodate them. We should, of course, do the same for their needs. Boundaries are only an issue when one partner abuses the trust of a boundary and uses the space given to harm the relationship. Imbalances in a relationship may be common with sensitive sensation seekers as we seek to give without adequately addressing our needs. Knowing what your needs are and adequately communicating them with your partner, while not allowing yourself to be manipulated or abused is key to establishing and maintaining boundaries.

Key Takeaways

- Love is more than passionate; it is also companionate and should transition from more unstable forms to more stable forms in healthy, long-term relationships.
- Knowing our attachment style is crucial to understanding our potential behaviors in a relationship.
- Relationships for sensitive sensation seekers may be quite a difficult issue as we balance the competing interests of our traits. Finding a compatible partner is more about finding similarities than opposites if the long-term future is the goal.
- Sensation seeking may be a great help in enabling us to "push through fear." It may be helpful to think of sensation seeking as that "wild friend" always taunting/inviting us to do things we would

never otherwise do. Pushing through fear is a growth opportunity potentially leading us to fuller, richer lives by extending our boundaries and challenging anxiety.
- Sexuality for the sensitive sensation seeker may entail quite a push/pull dynamic as we seek out new and novel experiences for the rush but possibly tempered with our emotional need to connect deeply with our partners.
- The "wild side" of the sensitive sensation seeker may open us up to areas of life unknown and unexplored by others. We should however listen to and honor our sensitive side in keeping us from harm and other risks that may destroy our lives.

Chapter 5
Self-Care

"If you want to live an authentic, meaningful life, you need to master the art of disappointing and upsetting others, hurting feelings, and living with the reality that some people just won't like you. It may not be easy, but it's essential if you want your life to reflect your deepest desires, values, and needs." –Cheryl Richardson, The Art of Extreme Self-Care: Transform Your Life One Month at a Time

Much has been written about the need for a serious approach to self-care for highly sensitive people and the same is true for sensitive sensation seekers. We may often find ourselves seeking new and novel experiences that indulge the sensation seeker but tire the sensitive part of ourselves. The see-saw struggle back and forth to accommodate all aspects of ourselves requires more than lip service to caring for ourselves in a holistic sense. Effective, sustainable self-care allows us to not only continue enjoying and experiencing life in all its richness and variety it also helps us develop our true potential overall as complex human beings capable of tremendous personal and spiritual growth. In this chapter, we will cover a number of aspects that are relevant to developing such a self-care approach and tailoring it to the needs of sensitive sensation seekers.

In my previous book: *Thrive: The Highly Sensitive Person and Career* I included a chapter on self-care as well articulating a holistic stance of self-care to meet our physical, emotional, and spiritual needs. In this book, I vary that theme to encompass the reality of the differences between being sensitive and being a sensation seeker. While sensitive sensation seekers and sensitive people both have to care quite assiduously for the side that gets overwhelmed on occasion and needs quiet to recharge. The sensation seeker equally has some specific needs that should not be ignored. Let's look at some of the considerations of sensitive sensation seekers.

Caring for the sensitive self

The sensitive self needs rest! Absorbing and processing all stimulation more deeply than others is a tiring affair for the body and mind. As highly sensitive people we need to ensure we actively manage our daily energy budgets by knowing our limits, setting boundaries, and assiduously attending to such simple things as hydration, appropriate levels and types of physical exercise, and the stimulation we are exposed to. In many cases, stimulation is simply in front of us without our choosing it. At other times we choose inappropriate stimulation (negatively stimulating) and feel our bodies and minds react with feelings of anxiety, agitation, fatigue, even disgust (as the news presents us images of death, war, and chaos).

Our sensitive selves notice subtleties others overlook, and we are built to think and feel deeply fueled by quick emotions. We are innately creative and capable of great innovation in thought and action. Sensory processing sensitivity as an evolved psychological mechanism is very simply an aid to survival for the species that likely developed at a point in our history when such a trait provided a survival advantage for the overall group. It is costly from an energetic standpoint requiring more use of our reflective capacities and cognitive processing, but the payoffs are significant regarding creativity, good planning, and adept interpersonal empathy. With this in mind, how can we best tend to our sensitive natures?

Thrill

<u>Our Emotional Selves</u>

Sensory processing sensitivity is a personality trait that works by utilizing quick emotions as the fuel that triggers more elaborate processing of all stimuli. These quick emotions, combined with high empathy, represent a sometimes chaotic inner life that may not only be quite troubling for us, but for those around us. Learning to manage our emotions and the resulting behaviors that become expressed in the world may be quite a difficult task in a world that seems to deny the inner life of the individual in favor of the outer social world of distraction, superficiality, and lack of intimate connection. How can we learn to care for our emotional selves?

Self-awareness

The first and most important step is developing a higher awareness of who we are, what makes us up, and what influences us. Self-awareness may seem ridiculously simple. Aren't we all self-aware? That is a question I often ask as I witness the seeming lack of empathy in the world. Self-awareness for the sensitive person involves understanding and appreciating that we will not always react as others do in a given situation. *Self-awareness involves an awareness that there is nothing wrong with us.* Sensory processing sensitivity isn't a disorder or an abnormality of any type. Very simply it is a marginally rare personality trait that interacts with a person's social environment and is moderated by personal choice, childhood experiences of support or non-support, and cultural context. Thus, HSPs may find life easier in some regions than in others and may experience vastly differing expressions of the trait. Becoming aware of how these factors have affected our expression of the trait is key to understanding and accepting ourselves.

Self-Care

"The highly sensitive side finds people a little bit frightening. When my Mom used to hug me, I felt like my skin was on fire. I didn't like her too close to me or anything. That happens with strangers too. I can feel them when they're too close. That high sensitivity just picks up on people's moods, and I take it wrongly as they are against me. I wish people could respect my boundaries most especially the touch thing. It's very uncomfortable for me. I wish they'd understand it's not the same sensation for me. It makes my skin feel very off. I wish people would ask more questions about it and make it less hidden, so it's better understood and not think we're weak or anything like that. It's just a different way of experiencing things. I wish people could learn from HSPs how to be more conscientious in dealing with other people." –Claire

"I always had these boundaries I was setting without knowing it. I knew who was safe and who wasn't. I had a very strong sense of empathy. I tune into myself daily through prayer, through meditation, through nature to really be in tune with my overall HSP self." – Jacquelyn

"I'm 56 years old and finally asking who I am. I realized "I'm not crazy! There's lots of people like me!" –Stephanie

"Society at large doesn't really feed me: when I'm with other HSPs, I'm in this swimming pool of acceptance of the difference and not beating myself up over not being able to cross the distance anymore. I try to keep some balance with it and see it just as different, not better, not worse." – Danny

"I'm always engaged in the process of reconciling what I know of myself to what I have learned of sensitivity. Often I can see why I chose to avoid certain situations or better understand why I am feeling angry, anxious, or sad. It works the other way too! When I'm feeling happy, *motivated, or enthused it's usually because another person has inspired me with their energy or example. I know now there are some types of people I want to keep out of my personal boundaries (or at least limit my exposure to) and those who I want to be very open to. There's a vulnerability in that, but it's usually worth it."* –Matt

<u>Setting boundaries</u>

Highly sensitive people have been described in some unique ways. One of the most interesting is psychiatrist Ernest Hartmann's view of those who he describes as having thin boundaries (as opposed to thick) in the mind where "high intake of sensory stimulation; awareness of thoughts and feelings combined; experience of in-between states of consciousness (daydreaming, fantasy); awareness of past blended with present; inclusive sexual identity, and transient group membership status" represent "a defensive and possibly adaptive dimension of personality."[33]

In Hartmann's view, those of us with thin boundaries are "especially sensitive, open, and vulnerable...we may react more strongly to sensory stimuli...we are more sensitive to physical pain...may become stressed or fatigued due to overstimulation...may be more allergic with more reactive immune systems...and may be more deeply affected by events in childhood."[33] Hartmann created the Boundary Questionnaire to allow us to determine how thin or thick our boundaries are. That may be found at http://www.youremotionaltype.com/boundaries/quiz.html. Full disclosure: I have taken the questionnaire and ended with a score of 59, which places me firmly in the thin boundary category. Not a bad place to be for a researcher/author/educator, but not a good place (at least in Hartmann's view) if I wished to be a salesperson or a lawyer.

There are other kinds of boundaries of interest to us as HSPs: they are boundaries (or limitations) that we can set that may act as defenses preventing some types of potentially damaging stimuli from breaching our "thin" boundaries. Understanding that we need to set a boundary in our mind means we have probably encountered a situation where we have been unpleasantly stimulated (a line has been crossed) necessitating a reappraisal of what we are willing and able to accept as appropriate. In that sense, the boundary is for incoming stimulation. Limiting the amounts and types of incoming stimulation, along with having a plan for how to respond if a boundary is crossed, will go a long way toward preventing overstimulation. This may not be easy or pretty, but it is absolutely necessary if we are to effectively minimize overstimulation.

Pause and reframe

Try as we may it's almost inevitable something (or someone) is going to set off our quick emotions and throw us into that awful state where just "letting it all go" would be such a blessing. At these times when the emotions have set off a chain of thinking and feeling processes that will not stop for minutes, hours, even days our instincts tell us it will pass in time, but the sense of overwhelm and activation in the body and mind are too incredibly intense (and often uncomfortable) to imagine it ever will. We should just settle down and relax right? Unfortunately, it's not that easy for sensitive sensation seekers. The feelings may be just too strong, the emotions too overwhelming to contain them in a box, or our bodies are so stimulated that we manifest the arousal as an inability to sit still or calm ourselves. In such times we can either find ourselves at the mercy of these powerful forces or we

Thrill

can begin to use our minds in the process of *pausing and reframing*.

The pause (withdrawal from the source of overstimulation) allows us to de-escalate from the strong emotions and relax our bodies, while the reframing part puts our minds back in the game. We can begin to question what we're feeling, why we're feeling it, and if it's logical and correct to have these feelings. We can search for alternative viewpoints from which to reevaluate the situation. Many times we may find that the quick, strong emotions precluded any rational thought processes and clouded our judgment. Once we have reframed how we think of a situation, we may well have removed the formerly strong emotion attached to it. Practice this technique the next time you feel yourself escalating toward overwhelm. Pause and reframe, pause and reframe.

We can also limit outgoing stimulation or the ideas, emotions, and energies that we put forth onto others. Knowing the effect we are having on others too often gets overlooked, yet what we say and how we project it energetically contributes to keeping us balanced while limiting how we affect others. *Managing emotional responsiveness and quick emotions will always be a tricky issue for sensitive sensation seekers*, but we can choose whether we act on a feeling or simply observe it, knowing it will likely pass. The immediacy of strong, quick emotions may make it seem otherwise, but that is where there is a greater need on our part as sensitive sensation seekers to know ourselves and our tendencies.

"I recognize how I'm feeling now and either take that seriously or don't act on it. At work, I never let how I was feeling get in the way of what I had to do. It never occurred to me I could do that for the rest of my life too. I've made so many choices based on protecting myself from

overstimulation. I've since learned that maybe 95% of that overstimulation is my thinking about what's going on. The sensitivity is there, and I need downtime, but it's just not the big deal it was a few years ago." –Nicki

"We really need to listen to our intuition and know when it's dead on because that's your clues to tell you how to plan out your day and go about your interactions with people." – Hannah

"It is about having a context now, and I now understand why there was so much emotion with that situation. I mean, for me it has given me so much more confidence and just to be myself. I think it is critical." –Bruce

"It would take almost nothing to set me off. Even now people say "you are the most sensitive guy I have ever met!" There are two parts to that. There is the part where I was leading a conscious life and not aware that these things are going on, and there is the part of me that learned to accept eventually that I was a highly sensitive person, and I have been trying to modify my life around that. It is the lack of self-knowledge that is creating all the problems out there in the world. People don't know who they are or what they are doing so they are creating chaos. I think if you are a highly sensitive person the only thing that is going to save you is self-knowledge. Otherwise you lead a totally crazy life." –Joshua

    Knowing who we are and how we function is one of the keys to working with our sensitivity instead of against it. As Joshua intimated knowing ourselves keeps our lives in better balance and prevents us from projecting out onto the world in a negative way. It may take years to effectively know ourselves and be able to recognize feelings for what they are. Understanding that we may simply allow them to exist without reacting may take even more time. Many highly sensitive people lead fairly chaotic emotional lives, and it is up to each of us to work on developing a deep understanding of our quick emotions and more elaborate processing of stimulation. As Nicki stated, *"I've since learned that maybe 95% of that overstimulation is my thinking about what's going on."*

Learning to judge whether our perceptions may be faulty is a learning process. *It is important to be patient with ourselves when we react poorly and be ready to forgive ourselves (self-compassion).* It is also important to reinforce our behaviors when we react well in trying circumstances. If we react well (or stick to a plan for how to react if a boundary is reached), and recognize that, it may be more likely we will do so in the future.

Focus on the positive?

With all the talk of emotional upheaval, managing strong emotions, and faulty perceptions one might think we would do better to focus only on the positive aspects of ourselves. The better question might be what role do pessimism and negative thinking play in our overall makeup? Does it have value or should we work to banish it entirely?

Contrary to some popular notions pessimism does have value. Being critical of a situation serves to engage our critical thinking capacities that entail reflection, looking at alternatives, and situating them in an overall context of meaning. The opposite is simply jumping in without thinking or reflecting on the wisdom of a particular action (and some actions can be quite costly or damaging).

Far from banning negativity and pessimism, we should cultivate a *healthy sense* of pessimism to counterbalance our instincts to make quick choices and decisions.[34]   Certainly, it's possible to go too far with pessimism, but a healthy balance where our inner skeptic is allowed his time on stage is an important part of making sound choices and is even more important to the sensitive sensation seeker because we are so prone to underestimating the risks involved to get the rush.

Caring for the sensation seeking self

The sensation seeking self requires care as well. It might be tempting to think that it simply takes care of itself, but there are some very real issues, several that we have touched on in previous chapters, that can impair our functioning. Sensation seeking may be a rather strong drive to seek out the new, novel, and exciting experiences, but when that need is suppressed it can be as unhealthy as taking undue risks. In effect, when we are holding ourselves back intentionally we are suppressing a part of ourselves that is especially rebellious about not being held back! Denying our nature in this sense may be risky.

Sensation seeking is most closely aligned with the openness to new experience on the Five Factor Model and overlaps with the same openness that highly sensitive people exhibit. As sensitive sensation seekers, our need to be open to everything new and novel is a need driven by genetics. It's literally "in our genes" to be out there exploring, challenging ourselves, and serving as a vanguard for our communities.

"What I love about New Orleans is the music, the food, the freedom. The last time we were there, we had tried so much food and been all over the city. At the room, I just totally passed out. I was done. The streets smell like piss and beer. I know I'm in New Orleans." –Stephanie

"From a young age I was always very curious about how the world worked, why people act as they do, and how I

Thrill

can translate my curiosity and openness to action in the world. I think there are fundamentally two kinds of sensation seekers: those who are in it just for the thrills and who do not apply it to anything and those who consciously choose to think and act in ways that are productive for all of us." –Matt

The best way we can care for our sensation seeking selves is to feed it, but without allowing it to run away with us! *Sensation seeking can surely be a tiger by the tail.* Sensation seeking, for the most part, seems to be mostly about external experiences and stimulation, but perhaps the challenge for us (as sensitive people) is to turn the focus more inward to a spiritually-oriented quest for inner growth and development in service to others. The combination of sensation seeking and sensitivity can be a powerfully charged creative spark of life directed towards the transcendence of biological type and cultural limitations if we so choose or it can be completely hedonistic.

Caring for our physical bodies

"To keep the body in good health is a duty...otherwise, we shall not be able to keep our mind strong and clear." Buddha

Taking care of our bodies should be the essential bedrock on which we build our lives, but all too often we ingest food and drinks that overstimulate us, offer no nutritional value, or at worst degrade our health and well-being. There is no one diet or way of eating that is best for sensitive sensation seekers. Our best approach is to tailor our dietary intake to our specific health circumstances and daily energy requirements. In some cases that will mean we consume a primarily vegetarian or vegan diet, in others, it may mean simply consuming a wide variety of reasonably healthy foods, so our bodies have what they need regarding vitamins, trace minerals and nutrients, carbohydrates, and protein.

Though many people object to one food or another as being unhealthy, the objections are primarily ethical and tend to homogenize all sensitive people together. *In fact, all sensitive people are not alike, do not believe the same things, nor do we subscribe to the same philosophies of dietary needs or preferences.* Sensitive sensation seekers may especially find it difficult to restrict our diets to one philosophy (due to our need for the new and novel), yet we should remain flexible and adjust as appropriate for our level of activity, age, and specific to our health conditions.

Hydration

Hydration is important in a number of ways. For those of us who take certain medications (like diuretics), it is crucial that we replace the water we excrete. Stress may also play a role in promoting dehydration as our often overworked adrenals circulate more aldosterone (a hormone that helps regulate water and mineral levels) when we are stressed. As the sodium leaves our body so does the water. Drinking small amounts of water throughout the day is better than large quantities all at once. Water is so important to our survival and health that we can only survive a few days without it. Many people think this means we have to drink quantities of water every day, but keep in mind we should count all of the water we consume from all sources. That includes water we get from soups, juicy fruits and vegetables, even tea, coffee, juices, and milk.

Exercise

One of the most crucial aspects of physical health for sensitive sensation seekers is exercise. There are a number of studies indicating not only the numerous health benefits of regular exercise, but also the emotional benefits including feeling better about ourselves, potentially interacting with others, and deriving the physical effects of dopamine release (a feel good hormone) in the brain.

The types of exercise we choose are important to our sustainable practice of the activity. Choosing something we like to do may seem obvious, but many people jump on the exercise bandwagon at the start of every New Year only to quickly lose interest. I propose we choose an activity that is simple and can be done just about anywhere: walking for instance. Walking is often underrated, but it's what our bodies are evolved to do. Our large, powerful legs occupy about half of our total body. The human species has spent more time walking than in just about any other activity (modern technology excluded). Walking is also so simple, requires no equipment other than decent shoes and it will get us out in the fresh air and sunshine.

Walking with a friend or with a group of people may make the exercise part of walking less noticeable as we busy ourselves in hopefully good conversation. At other times a solitary walk is the best medicine for clearing our minds and allowing our bodies to do something they are very good at. I think of it as a walking meditation though I don't worry about reciting a mantra or observing my breath. It is often enough to focus (or perhaps not focus) on simple movement, breathing in and out, and noticing the many sublime beauties of nature.

"Meditation has made a huge difference for me. Anxiety, nervousness, being able to reconnect with a spiritual practice has made a huge difference in my life. That would

be my number one self-care practice. Exercise is really important to me as is sleep. I changed my diet to a Mediterranean diet. I'm really interested in the connections between chronic fatigue syndrome, fibromyalgia and high sensitivity. I feel pain in my muscles and work through that with diet, exercise, and meditation." –Chloe

Care for our spiritual selves

"It is not the end of the physical body that should worry us. Rather, our concern must be to live while we're alive – to release our inner selves from the spiritual death that comes with living behind a façade designed to conform to external definitions of who and what we are." Elisabeth Kubler-Ross

Releasing ourselves from the kind of spiritual death Kubler-Ross described means we not only know ourselves deeply, but we understand the cultural context we live in and how that shapes and influences all that we are. The majority of people live in boxes without knowing it. What do I mean by that? I mean that culture is such an intangible force that we exist within it without knowing we are in it or that it is directly responsible for the words coming from our mouths as we espouse "our" beliefs and values. Culture is useful in the sense that it passes down hard-won knowledge that enabled past generations to navigate life successfully. It is not useful in the sense of allowing for an open-minded reappraisal of the meaning of life or of our place in it. If we accept the role that our respective cultures tasks us with we will have lived unexamined lives without conscious direction. Spirituality in that sense is a very human tendency to seek meaning in our lives through contemplating and enacting altruistic aims.

Thrill

Sensitive sensation seekers may be uniquely suited to searching for the greater meaning of existence because, as sensitives, we naturally prefer to think broad and deep about every issue allowing for an often open-minded exploratory process. As sensation seekers we often find ourselves pushing our personal envelopes, whether that be through thrill and adventure seeking or finding new and novel experiences both will provide a cumulative engagement and dialog with our inner and outer realities. It's very hard to climb a mountain and arrive at the top only to think superficial thoughts! What am I saying here?

The spiritual journey

I'm intimating the idea that *we sensitive sensation seekers seem to naturally find ourselves on what is essentially a spiritual journey as a matter of expressing our traits in the world.* Those long rides on the motorcycle to commune with nature? We're bonding with the all-encompassing oneness of nature, machine, and human being. That afternoon spent in quiet contemplation by the river? That's engagement with notions far beyond our own small existence. The walks on the beach while the ocean unfurls its endless waves against the sand? That's deep connectivity with eternity. Our own sensation seeking nature (the continual seeking of new and novel sensation) combines with our deep sense of reflection and thought to make us spiritual seekers at best. At worst we channel into destructive potentiality like addictions, risky activities, even criminal enterprise.

Being a sensitive sensation seeker by no means implies that we will be altruistic, community-minded, or even productive. There is a dark side to sensation seeking and sensitivity that can predispose us toward emotional upheaval and dysfunction if we do not learn to mitigate the types and levels of risks we are willing to take, learn to manage our own internal chaos, or deal with issues from our past. Spirituality may imply the practice of religious traditions with their attendant moral codes, but typically spirituality is thought of as separate from religion and broader in focus, though they overlap. However, many organized religions comprise repressive cultural traditions that inhibit the type of spiritual seeking I have articulated previously. If we are willing to simply subscribe to a preset tradition that supplies answers to any and all existential inquiry there is no point to seeking answers at all. Instead I advocate for the free and open-minded sort of inquiry we curious, creative people do as a matter of course.

Caring for our spiritual selves means we give purpose and meaning to our other struggles in life. Spiritual seeking is different from religious following, which is passive. *I advocate for a close and continuing examination of self and society, for the development of potentiality inherent in all of us as sentient, thinking/feeling, conscious beings capable of embodied action as individuals and members of communities.* Spiritual seeking implies we have to actively question the tenants of our notions of reality and uncover their manmade components. This does involve some existential risk as some people do not wish to feel "exposed" or to live outside their comfortable, secure worlds where things may be set in extremes of black and white, right and wrong, and good and bad.

"Sometimes it takes a bad life event to open us up to our deeper life needs. The breadth and depth of our spiritual journeys open us up to the distance we feel from our culture." –Danny

Thrill

The Buddha said we cannot live without a spiritual life, thus, it is in the search for a complete life that we give reign to the human need for meaning. In doing so we may actually find our truest selves. For sensitive sensation seekers the way we express our traits may make it likely that we become spiritual seekers who serve the purpose of redefining what it means to be human for our society, how we find meaning, how we connect, and how we should live.

"We open the collective conscious to the unconscious and tap the crown chakra of society. We tap it open to the spiritual dimension. Society could go on with science and mathematics and engineering and function perfectly, but what would be the meaning without journeying to all of the complexities of the soul?" –Danny

"I have an incredibly strong spiritual life and I've known for years that I am on a spiritual journey. I don't know the destination, but I trust the process." – Jacquelyn

"Through this process of having started and led a social group I feel this is my life's purpose. So where I'm going now is some sort of life coaching or mentoring. I'm tired of living under the corporate umbrella and want to be able to set the tone and do something that feels closer to my life's calling and helping people." –Chloe

"It's become a broader, more personalized spirituality that I have refined for myself. Spirituality has become quite core to my day without subscribing to any particular philosophy." –Robyn

*"I think meditation is essential. You can meditate in so many different ways. Find a way that works for you. It will help you center yourself and meditation is my culture. Find one that works for you and use that as a base. Then you develop into more complex and deeper forms. You have to

give yourself space, your own space. You need to give yourself time." –Ning

Journeying to the "complexities of the soul" represents but one of many possible paths we might walk as sensitive sensation seekers. What is clear is that we must first come to know ourselves very well so that we are operating from a center of balance rather than chaos. Too often sensation seeking overrides sensitivity with its ever-present need for new stimulation. Robyn explains *"I have often chosen stimulation over my sensitivities. Being stimulated has always been very important to me. I'm very easily bored by a lot of things, and I need that stimulation. It's been reasonably significant as a motivator."* Regardless whether we choose to focus on our spiritual selves, or our immediate realities self-knowledge is the key to living conscious, aware, deliberate lives where our developmental potential may turn into realized embodiment and action in the world. Caring for the vessels we inhabit (our bodies) while tending to our often chaotic emotional lives requires great fortitude, determination, and a looking beyond ourselves to find guidance along the way.

Our journey as sensitive sensation seekers may not be an easy one because we embody two very dynamic traits in a world that only seems to value the sensation seeking side of our personalities. Nevertheless, our ability to hold both traits equally within our one body holds tremendous potential for our growth and development, for our families, our communities, and our world. As evolved traits sensory processing sensitivity and sensation seeking helped our ancestors navigate the natural and social worlds. While we may less concerned with threats of predation (at least from animals) in our highly structured, ordered (even sanitary) civilization both traits still play significant roles in helping us predict the behaviors of others (sensitivity) and serve as a sort of *Star Trek* gene (sensation seeking) pushing the species forward to explore ourselves, our world, and eventually the vast universe.

In communion

We have talked a good deal about our individual journeys as sensitive sensation seekers, but not enough about the importance of communion with others. Danny mentioned the value of finding kindred spirits. There is tremendous worth in finding and spending time with others who are like ourselves. Knowing we are not alone can disarm some of the anxiety we may feel about being different than others. There's no better way to know this for sure than meeting others who are like us! There is also a feeling of kinship with like-minded people that goes beyond ordinary relationships. That sense of kinship can be extremely empowering in the same sense as our actual families are for many of us. Communion with kindred spirits can actually be a spiritual experience for many sensitive sensation seekers.

Self-care for sensitive sensation seekers means we move beyond our individual journeys and acknowledge and appreciate how we contribute to the groups we choose to belong to. There are some in-person groups that have formed the past few years (Meetup groups and others) as awareness has increased about highly sensitive people. These groups may vary a great deal regarding utility, but are worth a try!

Danny described the sense of communion as a "floating feeling" where one feels acceptance. That sense of acceptance is one most of us can use and derive great benefit from frequent interaction in. Self-care in an integral sense is a deep awareness of our inner and outer experiences with an emphasis on the growth and development of each person, family, community, society, and the entire human family. This vision may seem idealistic, but it's the same vision of Jesus, the Buddha, Mohammed, Martin Luther King, Jr., Gandhi, and other great spiritual leaders throughout history.

"The greatest disease in the West today is not TB or leprosy; it is being unwanted, unloved, and uncared for. We can cure physical diseases with medicine, but the only cure for loneliness, despair and hopelessness is love. There are many in the world who are dying for a piece of bread, but there are many more dying for a little love. The poverty in the West is a different kind of poverty -- it is not only a poverty of loneliness but also of spirituality." –Mother Teresa

Key Takeaways

- Care for the sensitive self involves emotional regulation, avoiding (or at least mitigating) overstimulating circumstances, and setting effective boundaries that both keep harmful stimulation out and prevent us from engaging in negative projection from within.
- Cultivating a healthy sense of skepticism is a healthy and useful habit. Learned helplessness is an extreme of pessimism, however, and one we should avoid.
- Care for the sensation seeking self requires that we allow it to "run free" at times, but temper it with caution, so we don't take undue risks.
- Suppressing our need for new and novel stimulation is denying our authentic selves.
- Self-care means we understand and appreciate our place in the world to develop our gifts, talents, and

- abilities in service to others. In doing so, we practice self-care on a spiritual level.
- Communing with others who are like us is an extremely valuable and empowering experience and one we should actively seek out.
- Our individual potential is for the benefit of all. We should embrace that potential and aspire to the fullest realization of who we are and what we can be for the sake of all people.

Chapter 6
Risky Behaviors and the Sensitive Sensation Seeker

"Don't be too timid or squeamish about your actions. All life is an experiment. The more experiments you make, the better." Ralph Waldo Emerson

The Risky Side of Sensation Seeking

There is another side to sensation seeking that is quite dark and dangerous to well-functioning in the world and certainly to our sensitive selves: risk and risk-taking. Zuckerman's describes sensation seeking as "the willingness to take physical, social, legal, and financial *risks* for the sake of such experience (varied, novel, complex, and intense sensations)."[9] Risk, in this sense, is voluntarily taken with the expectation of hedonistic rewards such as pleasure or enjoyableness.

High sensation seekers understand that there may be risks entailed in the activity they are contemplating and usually underestimate the degree of risk involved or are willing to accept them as worthwhile for the potential pleasure. Highly sensitive people likely overestimate (or estimate correctly) the risks in an activity and prefer to think it over carefully before making a choice. *Sensitive sensation seekers* may find it to be a sort of tug of war between the competing traits as we simultaneously desire to experience the stimulation, yet feel a commiserate need to carefully weigh the risks. In this chapter, we will explore risk, risky behaviors, and how that may be moderated by sensitivity.

Thrill

Evel Knievel?

As a young man growing up in the 1970s in a small town in Missouri, our neighborhood group of boys would often devise new and frightening tests of courage such as jumping bicycles over shoddily constructed ramps. It was the era of stuntman Evel Knievel making spectacular motorcycle jumps across the Caesar's Palace fountains, the Snake River Canyon, and numerous jumps across buses, cars, even a 20-foot long box full of rattlesnakes and two mountain lions! For most of the early to mid-1970s, my friends and I jumped all sorts of things on bikes not exactly built for jumping on ramps not exactly safe for jumping.

You might think that activities such as these would not be typical of a young sensitive sensation seeker, but you would be mistaken. I always knew the risks were high and the rewards low. The lump was always in my throat as I picked up steam on my bike headed towards a dodgy ramp to an uncertain fate. This period (the 1970s) was one before the internet, cell phones, computers, and all the electronic distractions that exist today. We made our excitement and were willing to take the risks until someone either got hurt, or it was time to go in for dinner (typically someone got hurt).

My jumping "career" later progressed to utilizing a mini-bike (a sort of small motorcycle) for one spectacular, ill-conceived jump on a hot summer afternoon. I had set up a very questionable ramp in the gravel alley behind my house and intended to impress the kids gathered around with expectant looks on their faces. Now mind you that a mini-bike is a powered vehicle with the ability to reach a good 25 mph or more. On this run I had the throttle fully on and zipped towards the ramp simultaneously thinking that "this may not be a good idea!" and "what an incredible rush!" I hit the ramp and flew off the end only to realize that my mini bike was built with a center of gravity that's towards the rear (not suitable for jumping). As I felt the tail end of the mini bike drop away (leaving me horizontal and hanging on for dear life) I felt the back wheel hit the gravel quickly followed by the front with a resulting catapult effect on my body as I hit the seat (or some part of the mini bike) launching me through the air and into the gravel.

I slid some 15 feet over the gravel and careened off of a convenient telephone pole (who put that there?) before sliding halfway down a water-filled ditch. The mini bike followed and glanced over me landing in the ditch. The kids thought it was the single greatest jump they'd ever seen! I, however, knew at that moment that I was not designed to fly so cavalierly through the air like Evel Knievel. I was relatively uninjured (except for assorted cuts, bruises and a great deal of pain, plus a limp) and pushed my mini bike back home (no way I wanted to ride at the moment).

In hindsight, yes, my sensitive self should have overruled my sensation seeking self, but it did not (I later drag raced cars as a teen) and does not for many people. Many of us launch off of metaphorical ramps throwing ourselves into some unknown adventure only to find we might have planned it better or at the least thought it over more. This is not to say that risk-taking presents us with no value. Indeed much of life entails risk of one form or another.

"I like doing things that are new, meeting new people, challenging myself. For about a year after my divorce, I tried all sorts of things like karaoke, riding bumper cars, Meetup groups, tried this, tried that. I tried mediation. It gets really tiring because you just keep doing that, but it

Thrill

was interesting. I felt more alive than I had in a really long time. I then realized what I liked, what I don't like, how much activity I can do before I get really burnt out." –Chloe

"*I like to go cliff-climbing and look for fossils in the ravine. It's kind of one of my riskier things I do because it is quite a steep dive. I like the feeling and thrill of it. I like the thrills like roller coasters. For a long time, I never had a fear of anything. I love being thrilled, being on the edge. I seek out thrills to get a big feeling in."* –Claire

"*I was a huge rollercoaster junkie, and we used to make these tree swings and swing out over 20-30 foot ravines. I dirt bike rode, I climbed trees; I was really a big paradox."* –Jessica

"*Very few people are as HSS as me: I hang glide, I skydive, kiteboard, I ride a motorcycle. I do public performances on my guitar sometimes. I'm a thrill seeker."* –Danny

Risk appraisal

Whether we are like Danny and seek out physical thrills or more like Chloe and seek out novelty and new experiences (remember sensation seeking comprises thrill and adventure seeking, novelty or experience seeking, disinhibition, and boredom susceptibility) we all accept risks based on what we anticipate being positive outcomes or benefits. For example, Danny knows that hang gliding, skydiving, kiteboarding, and riding motorcycles are fairly risky endeavors, but is willing to accept the risks based on the amount of pleasure/excitement he will receive. The level of risk we take is entirely subjective. Thus one person will judge the risks to be too high and the benefits too low, while another may judge the risks to be acceptable with the benefits worthy of the risks. The potential benefits coupled with our past experiences with similar risk tend to habituate us to risks if we find similar experiences to have come out well.

With risk come rewards. For thrill and adventure seekers it is the physical rush of excitement that flows through our bodies as we momentarily escape the normal limitations of our bodily abilities (a sensuous and freeing experience for sure). For novelty and experience seekers the risk is lessened, but nonetheless real for us as we push ourselves out of our comfort zones into unknown and potentially exciting territory. With both, we continually judge the severity of potential consequences while weighing our relative ability to control them. Determining the amount of control we might have in a given situation is exactly where sensory processing sensitivity comes into play as a mitigating mechanism.

"I will generally try to gather as much information as I can about a risk, so I feel comfortable about it. But, as soon as I decide, I do it. To other people, it seems impulsive, but I may have been thinking about for three months." –Chloe

"I essentially have two clear types of risk taking – one is more strategic and grounded which is the main type of risks I engage in as a sensation seeker and the other is more impulsive. My strategic risk-taking has actually been spectacularly successful generally in my life and represents many of my great achievements in my life. This type of risk taking is closely tied to my very finely tuned intuitive self (thanks to my sensitivity) and is a great indicator of many things." –Robyn

"We always do these very scary things together, but we're very calculated in how we take the risk. We're studying a lot more and not doing thrill seeking for its own sake. You're not going to see us take undue risks. We take smart risks where we do things safely. For instance, my

Thrill

boyfriend and I were in Las Vegas, and he was learning to play blackjack by betting small amounts of money to see how others reacted. They weren't necessarily good risks, but it was dipping his toes in the water to get a feel for the landscape of risk in that context." –Prisha

The sensitive sensation seeker diverges from those who do not have the trait (sensory processing sensitivity) in that we are much more likely to weigh any risks carefully before taking them. Being highly sensitive means we are keen to process our next actions thoroughly before taking them. This is the very thing that makes HSPs great planners!

The strategic risk taking Robyn mentioned represents the type of risk taking our sensitive side prefers to take, while the more impulsive risk taking suits the sensation seeking side (all sensation seeking involves some level of risk and impulsivity). For those of us who are sensitive sensation seekers we know the struggle all too well: we are presented with an opportunity that may not happen again or that we may have secretly wished to try, but never had the chance. Immediately our brains go into overdrive vacillating between a spur of the moment leap and more thoughtful reflection before action. A tug of war between competing interests (the sensitive need to minimize risk and the sensation seeking need to maximize the adrenaline rush) ensues that usually ends in the sensation seeking side winning out for many of us.

Taking risks for the sake of taking risks is not the intent of most sensation seekers, though for some the attraction to risky activities may make it more desirable. Remember we said that what the sensation seeker is really after is the adrenaline rush? The risk associated with an activity may enhance that sense of excitement.

"Much of my adventuring was for a rush. To fill the gap between me and the rest of the world with some kind of feeling." –Danny

Filling the gap

Many of the sensitive sensation seekers I interviewed expressed a high degree of dissatisfaction with the inherent superficiality that dominates our interpersonal relationships. As people who are "deep minded" we may find it difficult to connect in the deep, meaningful ways we would like and seek to "fill the gap" with sensation of some kind, any kind. In a sense sensation seeking can be a lifesaver for some of us because we have another side of ourselves we can turn to for stimulation when others cannot provide it (thrill/adventure seeking, novelty and experience seeking). Though our adventures may not replace meaningful, deep connections with others they may serve to at least round out our overall life experience. For some, though, the need for stimulation coupled with impulsivity and disinhibition/boredom susceptibility may lead them to try other forms of stimulation including drinking, smoking, drugs, sex, driving, and gambling.

The vices

Sensation seeking, impulsivity, and aggression are major factors in risky behaviors, the latter two to a lesser extent than sensation seeking. As a triumvirate of factors working together (in some cases) the risk of addiction may be high in some people. Zuckerman describes three motivating factors in the use of addictive substances "*curiosity* about their effects fueled by accounts of those who have used them; *pleasure*, a positive arousing effect described as "kicks;" and *avoidance of pain* or discomfort caused by attempts at withdrawal from use."[9] Curiosity is a trait we sensitive people have in abundance as we seek knowledge and insights into our world (articulated as an aspect of creativity in *Thrive*), but when directed toward drinking, smoking, drugs, and sex curiosity may lead us to experimentation.

Trying things

Experimentation is a natural part of life for most people. Most of us will have tried alcohol, marijuana, cigarettes and sex by the time we reach adulthood. Others may wait until much later. There is nothing inherently wrong about experimenting, but if it leads to addiction, it's a real problem. Sensitivity may moderate this to some extent as we pause to think about whether we are curious enough to try alcohol, marijuana, drugs, or sex, but as we've discussed the tug of war within ourselves often results in the sensation seeking side winning out. For some, this isn't the case at all, and we avoid everything in the list except sex (which we may perceive as relatively innocent in a relationship, but is in fact quite risky with random partners). Many sensitive people may be somewhat shocked to know how far sensitive sensation seekers will go in experimentation.

"I did Ayahuasca (an Amazonian entheogenic drug) recently, and now I'm more placed in the direction of my life. Before I was more full of doubts and scared. Since I did that now, I am more willing to do new things and feel changed. It is important to know who you are, where you are in your life, and why you're here, then to go for it in life. I would tell people to do what you need to do as long as it's safe and not hurting anyone. Life is short, and there are no

guarantees. I see now that I need to be less scared and paranoid and just go for it." –Mia

Mia also described how she has always been "really daring and dangerous" expressing the sentiment "I'm open just try me," but that while she would "love to go parachuting, bungee jumping; sports seem scary to me." Mia's disinhibition and the need for new experiences led her to try Ayahuasca, which may be mind-expanding for some people and seems to have lessened Mia's anxiety about new experiences. Many types of drugs or stimulants provide quick, intense rushes of dopamine (the neurotransmitter in the brain often called the feel-good hormone) leading to a state of intense pleasure, at least for a short while. Sensation seekers may really like this feeling and become addicted to the rush only to find they must use more (or different drugs) to achieve the same high as their bodies habituate to the drug use. The groups of friends we associate with have a great influence on whether we engage in the use of drugs, alcohol, smoking, and sex.[9] The more we are around other experimenters (or regular users), the more likely we will conform to group norms.

"I was around a group of co-workers who used alcohol and/or illicit drugs on a daily basis. While I found myself willing to try one of their drugs of choice (which I felt was relatively safe) and occasionally used alcohol I never liked the hangovers or feeling like I had compromised my own integrity in even casually using. The only thing I could do was leave the job when I was able. Realizing that I could have very easily become a regular user (even an addict) led me to greater understandings about my own character." – Matt

Matt's conscious choice to not conform to group norms of behavior demonstrates how sensitivity may mitigate sensation seeking. It might have been easier to conform, but Matt was able to compare his possible self with his actual self and see the new possible self (one regularly using drugs and alcohol) as unacceptable. The pressures to conform to group norms may be enormous and especially felt by highly sensitive people due to our higher empathy and emotional responsiveness combined with discomfort at being negatively stimulated (pressure to conform). John described his approach to conformity *"I am being who I truly am. That is more important to me than anything else. If they (society) do not accept that, I'm okay with that. I'll respect other people for who they want to be. Respect me for the same."*

Sensation seeking works through curiosity and risk tolerance. Though we may perceive simply trying new drugs, sexual acts or partners, smoking, or alcohol to be low risk stimulating the pleasure pathways in the brain (the same pathways through which sensation seeking acts in all likelihood) is seductive and appeals to many of us on a sensual level.

We highly sensitive people are able to enter altered states of consciousness more easily than others according to Swedish studies utilizing sensory deprivation tanks.[35] The use of mind-altering substances to enter altered states of consciousness may be to alleviate boredom, to fill in those blank spaces of time, or to derive the initial pleasure that comes with intoxication. Our desire to know what it "feels like" to alter our experience of reality plays to our high sensitivity, which already makes us feel "different" than others and sensation seeking, where our need for new and novel experiences may cause us to underestimate risk.

Questions and Answers

Risky Behaviors and the Sensitive Sensation Seeker

I use illicit drugs (mainly pot) and alcohol on a regular basis. Sometimes I don't know if it's because I like the feeling or because I'm self-medicating to deal with anxiety and worries. Will I become an addict?

Being a sensation seeker may make it more likely that you will try new things, including drugs, alcohol, smoking and sex, but is no indicator of whether you will become an addict. Moving from the curiosity stage to one of regular use is a transition that may happen without our being completely aware of it particularly if our social groups view regular use as their norm. This is where our sensitivity is an asset in imploring us to reflect on our choices. If we find ourselves using substances to avoid feeling the pain and fear of anxiety, it would be better if we found productive ways of directly addressing our issues. Substance abuse will only mask our problems and possibly make them worse because we fail to ever adequately address them or do any work on ourselves. Further, we set an example we may not wish to for our children or younger people who look up to us (not to mention the extreme financial, personal and legal risks).

I am often chided for taking too long to make a decision. I prefer to think it over before acting, and I usually make the right plans that are long-range in nature. How can I help others see the value of reflection?

It's true we live in a world where speed is often emphasized, and careful consideration is often seen as vacillation. The best way to help other people understand the value of your careful thought processes is to have a small success where you are proven correct. People's minds can change! Prove to them a few times how your sound reasoning and intuition is an invaluable asset and you'll be far more accepted for mitigating risks.

Thrill

I'm not sure if it's the risk I like or the rush of sensation I get at doing exciting things.

Sensation seeking, according to the research, is more about the rush, not the risk. The risk can make it juicy tempting for sure, but the real sensation comes from the experience being new and novel. In some circumstances, like those where we may not have access to healthy outlets for sensation seeking, the taking of risks may represent the actual rush of sensation.

Key Takeaways

- Thrill and adventure seekers enjoy the feeling of adrenaline rushes to replace or augment the stimulation felt or not felt through other people.
- Our risk appraisals are always based on risk versus rewards. We should always carefully weigh the risks so we understand the scenario correctly and avoid undue risks. Risk in and of itself is inherent in sensation seeking, but should not adversely affect our lives.
- Curiosity about many things is part of both sensitivity and sensation seeking. Experimenting with a variety of stimulation is, in most cases, healthy and growth-oriented. We should be extremely mindful though of how certain substances utilize the same pleasure pathways in our brains that sensation seeking utilizes due to the risk of addiction.

Chapter 7
The Creative Force Within

"There is a vitality, a life force, an energy, a quickening that is translated through you into action, and because there is only one of you in all time, this expression is unique. And if you block it, it will never exist through any other medium and will be lost." –Martha Graham

The Creative Instinct

The life force within each of us has been described in many ways, but here I want to concentrate on the life force as a creative force driving our growth and development. Creativity here is distinguished from the popular notion of creativity as simply producing an end product (art, performance, or written works) and instead envisions creativity as a creative "instinct" driving us forward in our explorations of our internal and external realities while providing opportunities for personal transformation along with our perceptions of reality.

This creative instinct propels us through life as very different individuals (as compared to the rest of the population) in search of the transcendence of our psychological type and biological inheritance. The sense of *being different* from other people is very strong in many sensitive sensation seekers. I suggest that one of the major reasons is due to this creative instinct that is never content with primitive expressions of what it means to be human and alive. We feel a deep need to define for ourselves what our humanness will be and how we will choose to use it.

To help us I will refer to a Polish psychiatrist and psychologist who spent over 30 years working with

Thrill

patients while he developed what he called a theory of positive disintegration. *Kazimierz Dabrowski's theory of positive disintegration (which we will shorten to TPD hereafter) is a multi-level theory of personality development focusing on moral behavior* with several key components that are of great importance to sensitive sensation seekers.

The basics

First, let's define what we mean when we say "personality." Personality for Dabrowski was not a given (as you might initially think due to popular notions and the definition I provided in chapter one), rather personality develops based on one's ability to break away from unexamined societal norms and values and develop a new sense of moral behavior that is a "self-aware, self-chosen, self-affirmed, and self-determined unity of essential individual psychic qualities."[39] Dabrowski developed his theory to explain what he had experienced of the "lowest and most depraved as well as the highest and most heroic" as he witnessed the cataclysmic events of World War One and Two. When Dabrowski was about 12, he witnessed the aftermath of a horrific battle near his hometown. He vividly recalled

"I remember a battle during the First World War. When the exchange of artillery fire ended, fighting went on with cold steel. When the battle was over, I saw several hundred young soldiers lying dead, their lives cut in a cruel and senseless manner. I witnessed masses of Jewish people being herded toward ghettos. On the way the weak, the invalid, the sick were killed ruthlessly. And then, many times, I myself and my close family and friends have been in the immediate danger of death. The juxtaposition of inhuman forces and inhuman humans with those who were sensitive, capable of sacrifice, courageous, gave a vivid

panorama of a scale of values from the lowest to the highest."[36]

Dabrowski believed that the majority of people (some 65%) exist in a state of primary integration (social level only) where they are largely subject to the rules, norms, and beliefs of their respective cultures. This segment of the population question little and show little personal autonomy in making choices or in developing at higher levels where a personal set of ethics guides one's choices and behaviors. At the level of *primary integration* people are motivated by the gratification of biological drives and self-interests. Little inner conflict is encountered at this level, though life still presents conflicts there is no transformative power in their resolution. Many may be highly socially conforming and materially successful.[37]

"The most important kind of freedom is to be what you really are. You trade in your reality for a role. You trade in your sense for an act. You give up your ability to feel, and in exchange, put on a mask. There can't be any large-scale revolution until there's a personal revolution, on an individual level. It's got to happen inside first." -Jim Morrison

At higher levels, people begin to act and behave in ways that are more autonomous, moral, and altruistic and less in ways that can trace their roots to unexamined conformity to societal norms and values. Dabrowski witnessed the worst and best in humanity and studied his patients over the next 30 years while he developed his theory of positive disintegration.

Authentic mental health?

One of the bombshells I want to present to you about this lowest level of primary integration is that *due to the cohesive structure Dabrowski would not consider these people mentally healthy*! Much like bricks laid solidly within a wall people in primary integration do not question their place within the wall or have room to expand or find a new spot. They remain as compact, neat presentations of a culture unable to significantly reflect on their reality or change it.[38] Throughout TPD we will encounter a very different notion of what constitutes authentic mental health that is very much at odds with Western notions of mental health as an "absence of disorders." Dabrowski's view of authentic mental health will factor prominently throughout this chapter and is perhaps one of the single biggest contributions of TPD to sensitive sensation seekers. By including this view, I want to reframe how we think of our often complex, chaotic, intense inner lives.

Disintegrations?

In TPD we experience *disintegrations* (which we know and recognize as anxiety, shame, and guilt) provoked by inner crises (emotions) that can lead to reintegration at higher levels of development (the positive part of disintegration) leading us to greater altruism, morality, and less egoism, less concern with fulfilling society's view of what our lives should be, and less focus on basic drives and instincts. *Not all disintegrations are productive or will lead us to development.* Some are quite destructive to our well-functioning and may lead to quite bad outcomes. For instance, emotions triggered as a result of self-interest are not growth oriented nor will they yield development. The theory of positive disintegration is, in essence, a no pain no gain theory whereby we do not develop if there is no emotional pain or "moderate imbalance" in Dabrowski's words.[38]

The creative mindset is one we know to be complex, fluid, and open. The creative instinct in sensitive sensation seekers may keep us in a state of potential emotional chaos at any given time, but it also serves to loosen our primitive inner structures that otherwise keep us from further personality development. The disintegrating/reintegrating processes so many sensitive sensation seekers experience doesn't mean we are unbalanced emotionally it means that we may live in a state of *positive disintegration* in service to our quest for a personality ideal. Positive disintegration, in this sense, is *a theory that places value on the sort of complex, messy, uncertain emotional lives we sensitive sensation seekers experience, rather than viewing this swirling inner milieu as a pathology.* That places TPD on a par with no other theory of personality development.

Another point that distinguishes TPD from all other theories is that progress from one level to another is not linear, and one level does not build on top of another. In TPD lower levels are broken up and left behind as we move between levels.[37] It is also possible that we, at times, regress and progress. There is no timetable for TPD, and the majority of people do not make it to the higher levels. Sensitive sensation seekers are, however, unique in certain ways that make TPD especially relevant to our lives. Germane to authentic mental health and leading to the next level is Dabrowski's description of the necessity of certain genetic endowments in a relatively small percentage of the population that exists in the form of what he termed "overexcitabilities."

Overexcitabilities

"People with strong developmental potential "must have much more time for a deep, creative development and that is why [you] will be growing for a long time. This is a very common phenomenon among creative people. Simply, they have such a great developmental potential, 'they have the

Thrill

stuff to develop' and that is why it takes them longer to give it full expression."[39] –Kazimierz Dabrowski

The right stuff for development

Overexcitabilities may seem like a strange term, but Dabrowski means that some of us are endowed genetically with certain forms of (in his words) "nervousness." "Nervousness. Enhanced psychic overexcitability (the literal translation is superstimulatabilities) in the form of excitability of movement, senses, affect, imagination, and intellect. Nervousness does not in any way entail the impairment of mental functions."[39] Overexcitabilities, or OE's, include five distinct categories:

- *Imaginational*. The inventive, creative, imaginative drive within.
- *Intellectual*. The reflective, curious, inquisitive drive to know.
- *Emotional*. The deep, empathic drive that connects us to others through emotional experience.
- *Sensual/Sensory*. The exquisite experiencing of sensory stimulation through the senses.
- *Psychomotor*. The expression of excited energy through bodily movement.

"Each form of overexcitability points to a higher than average sensitivity of its receptors. As a result, a person endowed with different forms of overexcitability reacts with surprise, puzzlement to many things, he collides with things, persons and events, which in turn brings him astonishment and disquietude. One could say that one who manifests a given form of overexcitability, and especially one who manifests several forms of overexcitability, sees

reality in a different, stronger and more multisided manner. Reality for such an individual ceases to be indifferent but affects him deeply and leaves long-lasting impressions. Enhanced excitability is thus a means for more frequent interactions and a wider range of experiencing."[39]

High developmental potential

In positive disintegration those who have emotional, intellectual, and imaginational OE's have what he termed *high developmental potential*.[37] As in the quote above those of us with high developmental potential experience life more deeply with life events not passing unnoticed, without deep reflection on their value to our lives, or without challenging our notions of who we are and who we wish to be. *Positive disintegration isn't just a theory of personality development it's a way of being where we experience conflicts, tensions, and frustrations potentially leading to advanced personality development toward a personality ideal that necessitates we leave behind lower level expressions of ourselves.*

Concurrent with deep experience is a certain amount of emotional upheaval, inner chaos, and anxieties and depressions. *Dabrowski believed that what we term disorders (in many cases) are in fact quite necessary for advanced personality development*.[38] He does acknowledge that true mental illnesses exist and are detrimental to the well-being and functioning of afflicted people, but the loosening of psychic structures that takes place when we are in chaos is a disintegrative process is healthy and normal in most cases. Without these disintegrative processes, there can be no real advancement of our fundamental humanness because in a state of equilibrium we never have reason to reevaluate our current state or envision a possible future self.

147

Thrill

Fundamentally, authentic mental health is a state of moderate imbalance.[40]

How does this apply to sensitive sensation seekers?

As I began exploring sensation seeking as a trait within myself and others, I decided to begin collecting data that would help me better understand the extent to which (if any) we exhibit OE's. To that end I embedded a self-test within a survey I asked only HSPs to take in 2014 (1,551 HSPs eventually took the survey).

The self-test was the Overexcitability Questionnaire Two, which is a standard measure for assessing OE's in groups of people. The OEQ2, as we'll call it, posed questions assessing each of the five dimensions of overexcitability: intellectual, imaginational, emotional, sensual, and psychomotor. Test takers selected responses from "very much like me" to "not like me at all." The results?

On the OEQ2 inventory, we tend to score *higher* on the intellectual, imaginational, and sensual items and *much higher on the emotional item*, but lower on the psychomotor item. What does this mean? It means that we have (at least for the 1,247 people who took this survey) high OEs in what Dabrowski called the "richer" items: especially so for the emotional OE. Overexcitabilities are one major component we need for advanced personality development and are largely determined by genetics (inherited).

"Enhanced excitability, especially in its higher forms, allows for a broader, richer, multilevel, and multidimensional perception of reality. The reality of the external and of the inner world is conceived in all its multiple aspects. High

overexcitability contributes to establishing multilevelness, however in advanced development, both become components in a complex environment of developmental factors."[41]

The Big Three and Developmental Potential

The results of the OEQ2 indicate that many of us seem to have the three OE's (intellectual, imaginational, and emotional) Dabrowski described as the "richer forms" that, if they appear together, give rich possibilities of advanced personality development and creativity. This does not guarantee that those who have high OE's will undergo advanced personality development or arrive at the highest level of humanness (secondary integration), but it does express in a very cogent way a valuation of our OE's and place them within a framework where we can begin to understand and appreciate them in what may be terrifically difficult, complex lives.

In addition to OE's Dabrowski believed that two other factors are crucial for advanced development: special abilities and talents and what he termed the "third factor." Special abilities and talents may be quite familiar to us because most of us are creative people with either realized talents or we are in the process of cultivating our talents and abilities. Creativity, though it may be used to produce art, performances, or other external expressions of imagination is fundamentally an instinctual drive to absorb and reinterpret concepts, ideas, and inspiration in deeply personal means and modes of expression. *I challenge us here to begin to think of creativity as a higher order drive that we may turn inward <u>reinventing ourselves</u> at higher levels of complexity, morality, and autonomy.* In Dabrowskian terms, the third factor represents a drive toward autonomous development many of us are familiar with and have felt in our lives as we experience a strong drive to develop our version of a critically examined sense of self that often differs from our society's homogenized, limited version of "selfhood."

"The instinct which creates the arts is not the same as that which produces art. The creative instinct is, in its final analysis and in its simplest terms, an enormous extra vitality, a super-energy, born inexplicably in an individual, a vitality great beyond all the needs of his own living - an energy which no single life can consume. This energy consumes itself then in creating more life, in the form of music, painting, writing, or whatever is its most natural medium of expression. Nor can the individual keep himself from this process, because only by its full function is he relieved of the burden of this extra and peculiar energy - an energy at once physical and mental, so that all his senses are more alert and more profound than another man's, and all his brain more sensitive and quickened to that which his senses reveal to him in such abundance that actuality overflows into imagination. It is a process proceeding from within. It is the heightened activity of every cell of his being, which sweeps not only himself, but all human life about him, or in him, in his dreams, into the circle of its activity." Pearl S. Buck, Nobel Lecture, 1938

Dynamisms at work!

To this point, we have described how some people have high developmental potential placing them potentially on a path to advanced personality development in search of a personality ideal where the constraints of culture and biology no longer determine behaviors. In place of society's structure, a new structure evolves that is self-constructed with a strong set of values guiding and directing altruistic behaviors in service to others. What we

The Creative Force Within

have crafted is a picture of growth and development fueled by moderate imbalance and a creative instinct that winds its way through our rather complex, messy lives. Dabrowski wrote that there are inner forces that are quite autonomous that fall into two categories: dissolving and developmental.[42] He called these inner forces *dynamisms* and described them as "constellations of instincts, drives, and intellectual processes combined with emotions."[39]

Dissolving dynamisms

Dissolving dynamisms operate within us to loosen the otherwise strong societal structures within causing us to question ourselves and the structure we live in. The creative instinct we have described busily invents new value structures as we break up and discard old structures. This process is similar to what teens experience in adolescence as they move from childhood to a more adult set of values. *The difference being that we need OE's (emotional, intellectual, and imaginational), special talents and abilities, and the third factor (conscious choice) to transform from dissolving dynamisms to developmental dynamisms.* If we have sufficient levels of the above factors, we create new mental structures of organization aided by our strong empathy.

Developmental dynamisms

As we might expect dissolving dynamisms are not sufficient to allow us to progress very far on our paths. Much as the adolescent eventually acquires new mental structures allowing them to function at a level beyond themselves in TPD we may move beyond the intensely negative emotions associated with conflict in the internal and external realms to greater self-awareness, self-control, and potentially syntony (attunement to the same vibrations as others), and auto psychotherapy. As we destroy lower level structures rooted in self-interest and replace them with value-laden, altruistic structures, we also become capable of greater self-care including the ability to engage in a self-improvement process that includes self-education and guiding ourselves through periods of stress and crises as our own counselor and therapist (auto psychotherapy).

"There's a large role for the contemplative approach that would rather listen to a hundred different perspectives and try and connect the dots and allow their inspiration to come in. That's what creativity is; it's those aha moments that happen universally. They want to have step by step guide to intuition; it doesn't work like that, it's much more non-linear. Step one is: clear your mind, good luck with that. There's this premise we have to address real world problems. No, we have to address real world people! It's the people who have to address the problems. It's true these issues are systemic, but they are being implemented by people: the drivers of the machines. We're too focused on the machines: it's not really the issue. My opinion." –Guy

"As far as just being very interested in people's lives and I think it is easier to look back and reframe it now and say now I understand the emotions I was going through because I am more aware now of the emotions that I took on because of the family dynamics and, at times, kind of being depressed because of all the family dynamics going on. Now I understand that, but back then I was just kind of not really understanding, but I think I enjoy being with people as well. The darker side is what I kind of pulled towards as far as my childhood because I am very much aware of other people's emotions. For me, instead of being tight down the middle emotionally, not to be open to expressing the emotions from anger to joy and everything in between." –Bruce

The Creative Force Within

"I have a very primal motivation that I don't want other people to have the childhood I had. I don't want people to have the life I have had. That underlies an enormous amount of what I do. I was treated in very unfortunate and unpleasant ways, and I will be damned if I will let that happen to anybody else. There is a huge protective streak. There is a huge sense of wanting to make life better, and there is a huge sense that each of us has something of importance. I spent a lot of time being told that I was oversensitive, and that I was immature, and that I was this, and I was that. All of these things have created a person who is generally speaking is pretty damn empathic and can walk in other people's shoes and help other people out and let other people see another perspective." –Samantha

"My vision for the long term is that we are collectively making a difference in the world and that a group who is fully realized in themselves, who feel confident and understand themselves and others and are willing to take action in whatever ways they feel compelled to do is going to make a huge difference. I'm a huge Star Trek fan, and I always think how we can get closer to a larger vision where poverty is eliminated, people get along, and people can live their purpose." –Chloe

"The best thing in society is we can help other people grow because we can read them so well. I think we need people like that with a different kind of mindset, a <u>different kind of creativity that helps the world</u>." –Claire

"The breadth and depth of our spiritual journeys open us up to the distance we feel from our culture. Sensitivity to me is an awareness that needs a function. Being around other sensitive people provides that function by my awareness looking at their awareness. I think society needs us more than they know, but they don't know that they don't know it. We open the collective conscious to the unconscious and

tap the crown chakra of society. We tap it open to the spiritual dimension. Society could go on with science and mathematics and engineering and function perfectly, but what would be the meaning without journeying to all of the complexities of the soul?" –Danny

The theory of positive disintegration is a complex theory that requires more study and reflection than I can reasonably provide in this book. TPD is, however, a very useful way of looking at our lives that I cite here because in all of my experiences interviewing sensitive sensation seekers I have witnessed positive disintegration at work in their lives even if they seemed not to be aware of it. I bring it out into the open here to discuss it in an open-minded way so that we may all benefit from the many insights it offers us. We don't usually hear about TPD largely because it doesn't fit society's view of mental health, it privileges those with high developmental potential, and it is a complex theory made more complex by some of the unusual terms Dabrowski used as descriptors (OE's, dynamisms, etc.).

Where do I fit in all of this?

Each of us is different, of course, but many sensitive sensation seekers will likely find that they have one or more of the overexcitabilities listed in this chapter. It's also likely that you're in tune to some degree with creativity and feel the effects of the creative instinct pushing you on to greater complexity, less egoism, and greater altruistic thought and action. You may also experience a good deal of autonomy in your thoughts and actions as you seek to choose your life consciously. Just reading a book of this nature means you are probably interested in many consciousness raising activities.

Where you fit, what level/s you may be at, and how Dabrowski's theory of positive disintegration can help illuminate our lives (lives that are emotionally complex, sometimes messy, and autonomous) will require more work on your part. I suggest viewing some of the many videos available on YouTube depicting Dr. Dabrowski speaking or any of the Dabrowski Congress sessions (and there are a number on different topics), or any of the well-written books on positive disintegration. I suggest considering *Dabrowski's Theory of Positive Disintegration*, by Sal Mendaglio, *Personality Shaping Through Positive Disintegration*, by Kazimierz Dabrowski, *Living With Intensity*, by Susan Daniels and Michael Piechowski, and visiting the website at www.positive disintegration.com.

The Overexcitability Questionnaire 2

Interested in knowing how you score on the OEQ2? Take the brief self-test below to find out. While this inventory has not been set up to enable scoring on an individual basis, you should gain a better understanding of how you score on items related to the five OE's: intellectual, imaginational, sensory, psychomotor, and emotional.

OEQ II Inventory[1]

Directions: Please rate how much each statement fits you. Respond on the basis of what you are like now, not how you would like to be or how you think you should be. Circle the number under the statement that most accurately reflects the way you see yourself.

1 = Not at all like me
2 = Not much like me
3 = Somewhat like me
4 = A lot like me
5 = Very much like me

1. I like to daydream. **1 2 3 4 5**
2. I am a competitive person. **1 2 3 4 5**
3. The varieties of sound and color are delightful. **1 2 3 4 5**

Thrill

4. My pretend world is very real to me. **1 2 3 4 5**
5. I am an independent thinker. **1 2 3 4 5**
6. I feel other people's feelings **1 2 3 4 5**
7. If an activity is physically exhausting, I find it satisfying **1 2 3 4 5**
8. Viewing art is a totally absorbing experience. **1 2 3 4 5**
9. I worry a lot **1 2 3 4 5**
10. I love to be in motion **1 2 3 4 5**
11. It makes me sad to see a lonely person in a group. **1 2 3 4 5**
12. I can take difficult concepts and translate them into something more understandable. **1 2 3 4 5**
13. I get great joy from the artwork of others **1 2 3 4 5**
14. When I get bored, I begin to daydream **1 2 3 4 5**
15. When I have a lot of energy, I want to do something really physical. **1 2 3 4 5**
16. I question everything--how things work, what things mean, why things are the way they are. **1 2 3 4 5**
17. I can be so happy that I want to laugh and cry at the same time . . **1 2 3 4 5**
18. I am more energetic than most people my age. **1 2 3 4 5**
19. I can form a new concept by putting together a number of different things. **1 2 3 4 5**
20. Sometimes I pretend I am someone else **1 2 3 4 5**
21. The longer that I have to sit still, the more restless I get **1 2 3 4 5**
22. Things that I picture in my mind are so vivid that they seem real to me. **1 2 3 4 5**
23. I observe and analyze everything **1 2 3 4 5**
24. I find myself mixing truth and fantasy in my thoughts. **1 2 3 4 5**
25. Theories get my mind going. **1 2 3 4 5**
26. I have strong feelings of joy, anger, excitement, and despair. **1 2 3 4**
27. I feel music throughout my whole body. **1 2 3 4 5**
28. I enjoy exaggerating reality **1 2 3 4 5**
29. I feel like my body is constantly in motion **1 2 3 4 5**
30. I love to solve problems and develop new concepts. **1 2 3 4**
31. I am deeply concerned about others. **1 2 3 4 5**
32. I delight in colors, shapes, and textures of things more than other people do **1 2 3 4 5**
33. I believe that dolls, stuffed animals, or the characters in books are alive and have feelings. **1 2 3 4 5**
34. Words and sounds create unusual images in my mind. **1 2 3 4 5**
35. My strong emotions move me to tears. **1 2 3 4 5**
36. I like to dig beneath the surface of issues. **1 2 3 4 5**
37. I am moved by beauty in nature. **1 2 3 4 5**
38. I am not sensitive to the color, shape, and texture of things like some people are **1 2 3 4 5**

39. When I am nervous, I need to do something physical **1 2 3 4 5**
40. I try to analyze my thoughts and actions **1 2 3 4 5**
41. I can feel a mixture of different emotions all at once. **1 2 3 4 5**
42. I am the type of person who has to be active--walking,
    cleaning, organizing, doing something **1 2 3 4 5**
43. I like to play with ideas and try to think about how to put
    them to use **1 2 3 4 5**
44. I am an unemotional person. **1 2 3 4 5**
45. I enjoy the sensations of colors, shapes, and designs. **1 2 3 4 5**
46. The difference in aromas is interesting. **1 2 3 4 5**
47. I have a talent for fantasy. **1 2 3 4 5**
48. I love to listen to the sounds of nature **1 2 3 4 5**
49. I take everything to heart **1 2 3 4 5**
50. I thrive on intense physical activity, e.g. fast games and sports. . . **1 2 3 4 5**

[1] Copyright, Institute for the Study of Advanced Development, 1999. (reprinted with permission)

Questions and Answers

I don't seem to be particularly high in any of the OE's. Does this mean I don't have good developmental potential?

No, not at all. People who are lower in OE's are still capable of living full, rich lives that are not wholly self-involved and that are well-considered and well-lived. Overexcitabilities are one component in determining whether we have high developmental potential. The other two are special talents and abilities (which any of us may have), and the third factor (conscious choice). The theory of positive disintegration is a theory that is big enough to fit everyone into.

This idea of authentic mental health is confusing. I've never heard that anxiety, depression or other issues are anything other than things to be dealt with by doctors and medications.

Thrill

What the theory of positive disintegration is saying is that these issues, when directed inwardly, may contribute to our growth and development. When they are simply reactions to the external world the effects may be temporary and lead us to no inner transformation. The words "moderate imbalance" are also key to understanding Dabrowski's view. <u>Severe imbalances</u> of any type are crippling to the person and any potential personality development.

I've heard of positive disintegration before, but isn't it only for the gifted?

Not at all. The research has been applied to the gifted population, but the theory of positive disintegration is a roomy enough theory to fit all of humanity into. The utility of the theory for us is in providing an overall framework of personality development in which we can contextualize our often unconventional, often non-conforming behaviors, thoughts, and beliefs while orienting us toward greater mastery of our consciousness combined with ethical actions.

Key Takeaways

- The theory of positive disintegration is a theory of personality development that uniquely situates our struggles as sensitive sensation seekers on a possible journey or pathway toward advanced personality development.
- Overexcitabilities are forms of "nervousness" manifested as bodily movement, imagination, intellect, sensory, and emotions. They are inherited in higher amounts in some people thereby providing them with one component of high developmental potential. They are the "right stuff" for advanced development.

- A state of "moderate emotional imbalance" is a necessary (and authentically healthy) component for positive disintegration to take place. People who are entirely stable have little of the necessary inner milieu driving disintegrative processes.
- The creative force within us can be a powerful drive that pushes us to dissolve less authentic expressions of ourselves and create newer, more authentic expressions.
- Greater self-awareness at higher levels of development should enable us to serve effectively as our own therapists (auto psychotherapy).
- Sensitive sensation seekers, as a group, exhibit much higher levels of emotional overexcitability than the norm and higher levels of intellectual and imaginational overexcitability. Thus, we effectively have one of the major components of high developmental potential. The other two aspects, special talents, and abilities and the third force, vary by individual.

Chapter 8
Living in Community

"What should young people do with their lives today? Many things, obviously. But the most daring thing is to create stable communities in which the terrible disease of loneliness can be cured." –Kurt Vonnegut

Socialization

In an earlier chapter, we covered some of the broad aspects of childhood that may affect the course of our entire lives. We said that sensitive people are more deeply affected by childhood events than in those without the trait and that sensitive people who experience childhood trauma also experience physical changes in brain development contributing to a number of issues with brain connectivity, higher set point of the default mode network, and activation of the amygdala (including the fight or flight reflex) in otherwise normal circumstances.

These long-lasting types of damage may be overcome to a large extent through efforts at relearning more appropriate coping skills and greater control of impulsivity and our overall mind "chatter," but their effects may be lifelong and hamper growth, development, and happiness. For those who experienced supportive childhoods, the opposite effect is true with sensitive people benefitting dramatically from positive support and feedback. Our deep emotions and thought processes work both ways. In this chapter, we will cover several key pathways that contribute to the varying ways we experience life as sensitive sensation seekers starting with the socialization process into the self.

Socialization into the self

The process by which we learn to become social adults happens through our interactions with members of our society. We bond with others who offer warm, friendly relations and feel a sense of security through which we further develop our sense of self. Socialization is that process and represents the way we learn the rules of our respective societies and groups.[43] None of us live in isolation, we all exist in many different contexts that we have learned throughout our lives including gender, race, and religion (to name a few). The socialization process continues throughout life as we age and join new groups. We are never finished with the process of learning what it means to be human.

Sociologist Charles Horton Cooley coined the term the *looking glass self* to describe the process by which society makes us human.[44] There are three major elements to Cooley's concept:

- We imagine how we appear to those around us.
- We interpret others' reactions.
- We develop a self-concept.

Based on how we interpret the reactions of others we develop a negative or positive self-concept. This process continues throughout life and, as many of us may have realized, we may misjudge the reactions of others. Our deep empathy as highly sensitive people combined with the way we process those thoughts, feelings, and emotions may lead us to overthink many situations dramatically and develop faulty notions of how others view us and negative, pessimistic opinions of ourselves. Highly sensitive people are especially susceptible to anxious, depressive thinking due to the depth of our reflection on events. Sensitive sensation seekers share this propensity in common with sensitive people with the added dimension of boredom susceptibility and disinhibition potentially leading us to impulsive, negative behaviors.

Our discussion of the theory of positive disintegration in the preceding chapter spoke of the necessity of breaking away from societal conditioning to a more personally authentic expression of ourselves laden with altruistic values. The power our societies and social groups exert over us in determining what we think, how we think, and how we behave cannot be overemphasized. Just like the bricks in a wall we are products of society and, just as solidly, stay in lockstep with expectations and rules of each group.

In effect, our minds and sense of self are largely products of society and the majority of people stay within the bounds of their respective social groups.[43] If they stray there are negative social sanctions (group disapproval, criticism, even disbarment from the group), while conformity yields positive sanctions (praise, acceptance, and approval of behaviors from group members). To break the socialization process and go against the grain requires a "different" kind of person!

Socialization into emotions

"It's important to remember that although a society may try to squelch some human attribute, it can never completely succeed. There is always some devious channel through which the disapproved trait can find at least partial release. There is a cooperative underside to competitive America, a rich spoofing tradition in ceremonious England, an elaborate pornography accompanying Victorian prudishness, and so on. Life would be so much less frantic if we were able to recognize the diversity within ourselves,

and could abandon our futile efforts to present monolithic self-portraits to the world." –Philip Slater

The way we learn to express our emotions occurs through our primary groups, comprised of face-to-face interactions with family and friends. This early intimate association produces feelings of belonging, identity, and how we view the world. These primary group perspectives are, of course, quite arbitrary and largely determined by broader societal forces. Depending on the beliefs of our family and friends we may learn it is acceptable to feel and express certain emotions, while it is unacceptable to express others.

All of these beliefs vary a great deal based on social class, ethnicity, and gender with each group containing a set of beliefs about which emotions are either acceptable or unacceptable. For sensitive sensation seekers, this early process of filtering out unapproved emotions may be quite damaging to our overall development as we wrestle with often intensely emotional lives, ones where now otherwise healthy emotions are disapproved of. What's the problem with suppressing emotions and feelings?

"It is a curiosity for me why society suppresses males so much emotionally: it is disturbing to me. I think it could release a lot of problems because that anger comes out in so many different ways." –Bruce

Whenever we actively seek to deny parts of ourselves, there is a commiserate push deep within us not to exclude that part because each of us seeks to be a whole person, not half a person. Carl Jung articulated the conceptualization of a Shadow personality that develops from these excluded segments of ourselves.[45] On a societal level it may be said that Anglo-Saxons (Americans) are predominantly obsessed with the control of emotional and sexual expression, but what do we see evident in the culture as a result?[43] Depression and anxiety are at epidemic levels, pornography permeates the internet, and elected leaders are often caught up in sex scandals (many times in same-sex scenarios they so vehemently fight against). Similarly, when we learn to hold in emotions, we push them into our Shadow selves. They will be back, make no mistake, and it is likely they will cause us much consternation as they seek expression.

"My parents gave me a lot of messages growing up to not be sensitive because they had suffered and it was their way of making me stronger. Now I know if I'm shivering it's because I'm overstimulated, it's just how I do things, it's not fear and perfectionism or all these other things." –Prisha

"My strong emotions, I think, scared my mother because what mother is willing to see their child stressed out? I think it was the intensity and depth to which I seemed to feel emotions that concerned her. She's an emotional person herself and seeing that quality in her child must have been alternately confusing and worrying. My father was fairly emotional under the surface but didn't display these emotions often unless he was activated by something. I learned that I had this intense, deep emotional life that was unlike other people around me. I didn't know what to make of it as a child or as an adult in my 20s. They just seemed to get in the way of being like other people, especially men. As I have gotten older, I'm more at peace with being who I am and have been more open with my children about their strong emotions." –Matt

"I suppressed a lot of my feelings growing up because I didn't want to rock the boat because of all my family dynamics; even seeing anger as bad, but now sensitive to me is just if I am angry to express it and get it out. Interestingly I have found that as I express anger and get

all that out, I can experience more happiness and joy on the other side of that too. For me, instead of being tight down the middle emotionally, be open to expressing the emotions from anger to joy and everything in between." –Bruce

"My father grew up in a generation where men were stern and quiet, just that generation of men, very strong and silent. I remember when I was little and started to cry it was that "shut up or I will give you something to cry about" thing." –Samantha

Learning that we should suppress emotions to please our parents (whom we often view as Godlike at an early age) primarily affects our sensitive side more than our sensation seeking side, but, since we process negativity so deeply rejection of healthy emotions may lead us to feel we are very different than others thereby setting us up for viewing ourselves as defective, abnormal, or cause us to turn another way that is more callous, hard, and unfeeling (at least on the surface). This may be especially true for boys as we learn conflicting messages about emotional expression: Don't cry, crying is only for weaklings! Suck it up Buttercup! Ewe! I don't want a man who cries!

It is true that, in some regions, the culture is changing as younger generations decide for themselves that suppressing emotions is unhealthy, unproductive, and unwise, but, in many other regions the culture still emphasizes a hard personality best suited for competition rather than cooperation and community. In these cases, we are left on our own to both learn to process our strong, quick emotions and decide whether to act on them. Emotional regulation becomes a necessary life skill in such cultures.

Emotional regulation

Managing our emotions is certainly no easy task given that we are hard-wired as sensitive people to experience strong emotions leading to more elaborate processing of all stimuli (the pause to check before acting instinct). However, there are some concrete steps we can take to make up for some of the shortfalls many of our cultures fail to provide:

- *We can choose not to act on emotion.* Just because we feel an emotion does not mean we have to act. We can just as well acknowledge the emotion and know that the strong feelings will pass in time. As sensitive sensation seekers, we prefer to address our emotions directly rather than shove them aside.
- *We can distinguish between emotions that are ours and those that belong to others.* Sensitive sensation seekers are strongly empathic, and we may be absorbing and experiencing the emotions of others as if they were our own. We need to cast a critical eye on an emotion and determine if we own it. This is the *pause and reframe* technique I mentioned in the self-care chapter.
- *We can tell others how we are feeling and in the ensuing dialog better understand why we may be feeling a particular emotion.* This may take the form of a trusted friend, trusted relative, or a skilled person like a therapist, counselor, or psychologist. Talking with others often lessens the intensity of the emotion as we bring it out into the open to examine. Doing so may lessen the duration of intensity and help us in the future to cope better with a similar emotion.

"As I have taken more ownership of my own emotions I know that when the fears start coming up, I can manage it so that it doesn't destroy me psychologically." –Prisha

Being in charge of our emotional lives is a topic of enormous importance to sensitive sensation seekers because so many of us do not learn appropriate coping mechanisms from our respective cultures. Since we all live in numerous social contexts and because culture is a constantly shifting construct being renegotiated by each of us we each share the burden of developing ways of managing our emotions and passing down that knowledge to the next generation (our children). Hopefully, we learn that our sensitive trait has value in our lives, in our families, and to our communities.

Conformity and the sensitive sensation seeker

In chapter 1 we covered the basics of personality and said that who we are is a blend of different influences ranging from the genetics we inherit to our social environments mixed with personal choices (the conscious choices of Dabrowski's third force). We also said that adaptations are evolved psychological mechanisms evolved to address specific issues when they were evolved. What happens then when we find ourselves with two adaptations (sensory processing sensitivity and sensation seeking) in modern highly structured, ordered societies?

For sensation seeking the answer seems to place us further from acceptance and social conformity and more toward autonomy and individual expression. For sensitivity, the picture may be less clear as our social groups are, in many cases today, less intact and dominated by those who do not seem to place a high value on empathy or depth of thought or feeling. The scarcity basis many modern societies operate on keeps many people unnecessarily tense, irritated, and hard on themselves and others. For sensitive people, we may already feel profoundly "different" than those around us and perceive that conforming to artificially, arbitrarily derived norms of behavior and values that do not fundamentally fit us denies who we are.

There is another part to conformity that may work in our favor: the outsider effect. When creative people perceive social disapproval and embark on our creative journeys to self-expression, based on our value structures, encounter new social disapproval we often interpret that disapproval as justification for our feelings of being different and may push on to greater achievements. In a nutshell, we cease worrying about social approval and begin to follow our paths more strongly utilizing more of who we are less of who we are not. This can be enormously freeing and liberating even if emotionally painful over the short-term.

"I did not used to consider myself a creative person, but now that I am my own self and stopped buying into the stigma of our society's message, oh yes! Now I do wire-wrapping, photography, playing guitar. I no longer concern myself with how others see me. I am free to be me." –John

"I didn't feel different until I was 15-16, then I never really felt similar to others again. In round two I found that I felt similarities to others who felt different. That was made different because it was lacking for so long. The breadth and depth of our spiritual journeys open us up to the distance we feel from our culture." –Danny

"I don't feel the need to be understood anymore. Sometimes people are thrown off because I'm freer and looser than I used to be or more comfortable with me because I'm freer

and looser than I used to be. I don't feel like anyone else needs to get me." –Nicki

The sensitive sensation seeker is likely to be far less interested in fulfilling other people's notions of what our lives should be like and how we should live them. The propulsive dynamics of boredom susceptibility coupled with disinhibition and the need for new and novel experiences means we are simply not people cut out for conventional lives of what Thoreau called "quiet desperation." *Quietly desperate is what we will be if we find ourselves on conventional pathways!* Many of you have felt the "pangs of desperation" as described by Danny when in unstimulating environments and have probably had to adjust your lives many times and with more personal upheaval than in those without the traits. Non-conformity for sensitive sensation seekers is more than a youthful way to pass the time while in college, it's a way of life whereby we find expression through the "devious channels" Philip Slater described earlier.[46]

"I've found that being a male HSP I have to look at it as an act of rebellion. That I have to let something go to gain something. I have to let go of the belonging to the collective male consciousness and come back at it from an outsider place and be guarded when I do it and bring with it the consciousness that I'm clearly not joining them; I'm leaving them. I need to for my own personal fulfillment and be the kind of person I am. It's a growth experience, and I appreciate the person I am more." –Danny

"I have always had a clear instinct that I was not cut out to follow the herd; that I was different in fundamental ways that precluded my existence at a superficial level. Finding my way has been the journey and struggle of a lifetime." – Matt

Thrill

"I find my two sides in combat with each other." –Claire

Authentic expression of our highest humanness, in Dabrowski's view, requires of us that we break with societies that present us with one view of life that narrowly defines who are and who we ought to be, or non-conforming autonomy. To be a sensitive sensation seeker is to be self-determined, tolerant of ambiguity, and willing to dissolve former versions of ourselves to make way for new versions.

Gender

"Star Trek was an attempt to say that humanity will reach maturity and wisdom on the day that it begins not just to tolerate, but take a special delight in differences in ideas and differences in life forms. If we cannot learn to actually enjoy those small differences, to take a positive delight in those small differences between our own kind, here on this planet, then we do not deserve to go out into space and meet the diversity that is almost certainly out there." –Gene Roddenberry

There are quite a few things that separate the way we experience life as sensitive sensation seekers, but none more so than gender. Gender is a means by which society seeks to control its members by assigning a *master status* that affects all facets of life.[43] Gender is the single biggest factor that separates the experiences of men and women besides social class. Gender is a socially constructed framework of arbitrary ideas that each society has developed over time. Thus, what it means to be a man in one society would seem entirely wrong in another. Similarly for women what it means to be feminine may be completely different from one culture to another.

"I definitely think it's easier for a guy to be HSS than for a woman because of social mores." –Carla

"My parents were less concerned about gender and more about where you are fully expressed. Gender for me is irrelevant. I never let it hold me back." –Chloe

"When people realize I'm more adventurous they are attracted to it because it's not as common in females." – Claire

"It is more acceptable in Sweden for a male to be a sensation seeker, definitely, I think so because we are living in a country that's pretty equal, but there are big differences still. Being sensitive is easier for a female." – Freja

"Though I was raised in a household with very traditional, macho ideas about masculinity I always felt more complex inside than other males because I have a deep emotional life that affects everything, and I always felt traditional males are quite limited." –Matt

Social control mechanism

Gender, as a social control mechanism that varies in expression from culture to culture, deeply impacts the way sensitive sensation seekers experience life. Depending on how high one is in sensitivity or sensation seeking will determine the exact nature of our experience. Thus, a person high in sensation seeking who is a male might find that he is more accepted in a highly competitive society like the U.S. but suffer in the sense of not being able to express his sensitivity fully. *Sensation seeking is a bulldozer that will quickly override sensitive impulses if given a chance.* This is compounded by a society that glorifies sensation seeking (especially thrill and adventure seeking) through the culture.

If we are high in both sensitivity and sensation seeking it is quite another dance. Two competing, diametrically opposed personality traits (adaptations that helped our species to survive in ancient times) seeking to find expression in one person indeed sets up a scenario of "moderate imbalance" in Dabrowski's words. For males being high in sensitivity AND sensation seeking can be a pressure cooker of pushes and pulls alternately imploring us to approach without pausing and pausing to check (reflect/gather more information).

Masculinity

"*Manhood is not the manifestation of an inner essence; it is socially constructed...it is created in the culture. Manhood means different things at different times to different people.*" –Michael Kimmel

Traditional notions of hegemonic masculinity demand aggression, risk-taking, competitiveness, stifled emotions, dominance over women, sexual prowess, and an outward appearance of "mastery of all things." Hegemonic masculinity must be "constantly demonstrated and requires proof."[47] This definition would be very hard for a man who is high in sensitivity to embody without losing the core of what makes him human, but many of us do it anyway (to some extent) because we live in the society and inevitably some of it will absorb into us through osmosis. This does not mean we become hard, callous, and unfeeling, but it does mean that it can be quite difficult to construct a passable "mask" that we show when required while managing a much deeper, richer inner life.

Sensation seeking in all likelihood is an easier trait to express in Western societies than sensitivity. There are reasons for this related to the above definition of hegemonic masculinity, but the one aspect of sensation seeking that would likely *not* be as acceptable is our boredom susceptibility. In Western cultures, the notion of being bored denotes a non-productive state associated with sloth, laziness, or personal weakness (which is deeply frowned on). Ironically, in our modern, interconnected, interdependent world traditional masculinity holds little (if any) value. The skills that are in most demand in the workplace and the society emphasize cooperation, mentoring, and creativity.

Navy Seals

One study, done by Jim Uhl, a former Navy Seal and researcher, gathered narratives from 11 former Navy Seals and explored the way these warriors, who have proven beyond all doubt that they could meet the litmus test of hegemonic masculinity, discovered and integrated qualities we typically associate with femininity such as empathy, caring, self-reflection, even vulnerability. What Uhl found was a completely different scenario than we might think would be typical of "warriors," but, first, let's look at types of masculinity so we can appreciate the nuances.

Uhl describes four types of masculinity: "*hegemonic masculinity*, the dominant form of masculinity in Western society with men who have embodied the stereotypical traits of masculinity such as being unemotional, tough, authoritative and controlling; *marginalized masculinity* refers to men stigmatized by race or economics in a dynamic relationship with conventionally hegemonic men; *complicit masculinity* comprises the majority of men who do not meet the ultimate expectations of masculinity, but who benefit from the subordination of women, lesbians and gays; and *subordinated masculinity* is experienced by gay men and viewed as the bottom of the ladder."[47]

The emphasis on cooperation with others is a vital component of a Seal's training and directly contributes to their success, but what happens after military service for these former warriors? Uhl found that the men he interviewed expressed a sense of having satisfied any demands of hegemonic masculinity as a result of having completed Seal training. With nothing to prove they felt freer to embrace and embody a new conceptualization of masculinity that includes feminine aspects like empathy, vulnerability, selflessness, along with a high sense of integrity and honesty directed toward personal authenticity touching every facet of life.[47]

What can we learn from this? First, we need to appreciate the extent to which we are conditioned to think how other people should behave according to their sex or gender. It's only through a deeply dualistic division of roles that we relegate men to narrow, limited, and unhealthy expressions of masculinity. Second, if Navy Seals (men who have fulfilled the ultimate in hegemonic masculinity) find that aspects of femininity serve them well in their lives both in and out of the military we "lesser mortals" should not feel threatened by following their lead and becoming the types of men capable of providing caring, support, and mentoring to those around us while "kicking it in gear" when we need to (it's entirely possible to be sensitive and tough). Lastly, it is only through our willingness as sensitive sensation seeking men to feel secure enough within our own selves that we can express a new conceptualization of *integral masculinity*.

Integral masculinity

Integral masculinity would replace formerly stratified forms of masculinity by an embodiment of a new model. The *integral male* would value his inner life as much as his outer; feel equally as comfortable with empathy as achieving a goal; be free and open enough with himself (and others) to allow himself to feel and express emotions;

value cooperation, teamwork, and community as much as individualism, toughness, and grit. In effect, integral masculinity coincides with the sort of conscious third force personal choices Dabrowski described in the theory of positive disintegration (see more in chapter 7).

Femininity

The definition of what it means to be a female in society is a story of historical patriarchy with men becoming the dominant sex likely due to shorter life spans at that time and the necessity of reproduction and child-rearing. Our hunter-gatherer period of human history may have been a different story with greater equality between the sexes, but in contemporary hunter-gatherer tribes, it is the women's consistent knowledge and ability to find and harvest staple crops that contribute *the most* to the overall diet. If a male hunting team makes a kill, it's a big bonus, but they often return with either no kill or only small game. Women have been making small gains for hundreds of years for equality in many spheres of life often meeting with much resistance from the dominant patriarchal culture.

The transition from an industrial economy to a knowledge-based economy has created new work opportunities for women but has also brought into question the feminine gender role. With over half of the workforce now female is it reasonable to expect notions of domestic bliss to work in the 21st century? How does this affect the sensitive sensation seeking woman? What does it mean to be a participant in renegotiating culture (which each of us is doing through our choices and espoused beliefs and values)?

Claire spoke of the attraction others felt to her sensation seeking due to its novelty. It's probably fair to think that others will be far more accepting of us as sensation seekers than as sensitive people (unless the people around happen to be sensitive as well or particularly open). Sensation seeking for a woman may distinguish her from others (those without the trait or who are lower in the trait) making her more appealing on a surface level, and that may open new possibilities for others to know her deeper self.

"I'm both sensitive and strong. They see my strength then don't want to see my sensitivity. I think even more difficult can be when someone sees my sensitive side, and they want to take care of me, and I'm like, yes, it's true that I can cry over one thing then the next day be very strong. I think if they could understand the variation within me and accept that and not take it to serious." –Freja

"It's almost like two different people. I like to drop f-bombs to make a passionate point, and sometimes I think "Oh my God, I can't say that!" Often I may want to say something that will be controversial and have a lot of shock factor, and I just withhold and keep it to myself. I love when someone else makes an off-color remark (like say a sexual joke), and people laugh uncomfortably. I never have the courage to do that myself, but I want to. I feel like I have to manage people's impressions of me, and that keeps me from expressing myself." –Jane

"Generally being a HSP is female and being HSS is male in the American culture. The HSS part of me that gets people going that gets them rallying around I don't think is that hard." –Eleanor

"Being female I think makes it easier to be sensitive. Being a sensation seeker is more difficult because it's perceived as more associated with males. On good days I see it almost as a yin-yang situation, just without the tension.

There are very good ways the two aspects of myself work together. I see them as being very gender aligned for me."
–Robyn

"I think I have always been really daring and dangerous. Growing up it was very much like you belong to a certain class and I never fit in with that. I always wanted to do whatever was possible to do at that moment. I'm a mother now and have two kids and have to be different with them than what I learned growing up. It's up to me now about how I can change that." –Mia

"I grew up in a time when girls didn't do that stuff. I was considered sort of the tomboy, but it was like "gosh, you shouldn't be on a motorcycle or a skateboard!" They tried to put me in dresses and make a girl, but I just had this aspect that I just wasn't ladylike. Kids now have progressed to a point where society is not so rigid anymore. People are easing up on that." –Jessica

As with masculinity finding or creating the bridges between ourselves and other people that can lead to greater understanding and acceptance of sensitivity seems to be the primary task. Sensation seeking as a trait is part and parcel of many Western societies, especially the thrill and adventure seeking, but also the novelty seeking and to some extent disinhibition whereas sensitivity is quieter and less acknowledged or valued in ego-driven, highly competitive social environments.

Masculinity and femininity will continue to evolve as each generation determines for itself what it means to be male or female. Today we see evidence of this in the greater freedom of transgender people to express their gender identity, though we also witness the pushback from the dominant male patriarchy.

Aging and the late bloomer

Thrill

"When you're young, you always feel that life hasn't yet begun—that "life" is always scheduled to begin next week, next month, next year, after the holidays—whenever. But then suddenly you're old, and the scheduled life didn't arrive. You find yourself asking, 'Well then, exactly what was it I was having—that interlude—the scrambly madness—all that time I had before?" –Douglas Coupland, Life After God

The same social forces that largely determine how we view our gender roles, our emotional lives, and our overall worldview also deeply affect how we view aging and ourselves as aging individuals. It's been said that highly sensitive people simply do not know themselves well enough until mid-life to achieve what others do much earlier. In several ways, that may be true. For one, sensation seeking tends to decline in intensity with age leaving only boredom susceptibility behind. This leaves us with the majority of our lives to work out how to live as highly sensitive people. That may be little comfort to many of us who have found it quite difficult to reconcile our deeply emotional, reflective natures with a world that often demands the opposite of us on a daily basis. How are we to view aging in that case?

We can acknowledge that our notions of aging are socially constructed and, thus, tied to the vagaries of our society. In the U.S. our society is obsessed with efficiency, productivity, competitiveness, and a limited view of the value of life after a certain age beyond vague notions of "retirement." Where does this leave the sensitive sensation seeker who has only come into self-knowledge at mid-life? I suggest we move from thinking of an industrial economy paradigm of retirement to lifelong engagement in personally meaningful activities and community engagement. This means we have to make a number of conscious choices that may free up our time to focus on the activities that feed our sensitive natures and less on those that do not.

There is a certain existential dread to aging many of us feel as we hit mid-life and begin to feel the effects of aging on our bodies and minds. What seemed like an infinite amount of time, at some point, becomes finite and limited. Our awareness of this reality shouldn't cause us to despair; rather we should make the most of what we have at any given point in life. We highly sensitive people are more prone to depressive, anxious thinking than in those without the trait (again due to the reflective nature and quick, deep emotions), thus it's even more critical that we map out a plan for aging as we near mid-life, one that will allow us to continue on our personal growth paths toward our personality ideal.

Being a so-called late bloomer (as I consider myself) means that we probably spent a great deal of time and effort earlier in life trying to simply get along in society while denying who we are or having it squished deep down into ourselves as a result of the demands of daily life. As we neared mid-life many of us began to lose our sense of obligation to the culture as our children reached adulthood and we sensed real personal freedom again. At the least, we perhaps worked in one or more careers and never quite found a place that "fit." *This is especially true for sensitive sensation seekers because we may be better suited to short-term projects than repetitive, never-ending routines.* We may have sensed this earlier about ourselves in various situations, but never had the ability to craft a uniquely tailored set of conditions that can make the most of this disposition.

People have asked in my consulting work if life is possible as a late bloomer. Many feel that ageism is strong in our society and opportunities few. That may be true to some extent (probably varies a great deal by the region you're in), but our ability to seek out and find engagement is never-ending and only limited by our drive and desire to serve others as well as fulfill ourselves.

Carl Jung said we spend the second half of our lives in search of spirituality.[48] Spirituality not in the sense of organized religion, rather in the sense of meaning-making in life. We have a unique opportunity in our modern age where life has been greatly extended through improved nutrition, medical interventions, widespread awareness of health, and improved healthcare. People in the 21st century are simply healthier than in past generations, live longer (on average), and have more time to focus on existential matters like the purpose of life, meaning-making, and building relationships that sustain us.

I have also been asked if returning to college in mid-life is possible, if it's too "weird," or if the work is too hard. My reply has always been that mid-life is a great time to pursue unfinished things that we may have started earlier in life or undertake new ones. My return to college at the age of 43 and subsequent successes were predicated on a deeply felt necessity to find a place in life where I could bring to bear my broad interests, skills, and potentialities. For me, that decision (a conscious choice) was one of the absolute best things I have ever done. The road ahead may still be one of frequent reinvention, but I am at peace with that and with the journey itself. The focus for me now is to stay fruitfully busy for as long as I am able or choose to be engaged. This flexible, far-reaching perspective affords me maximum opportunities while acknowledging my desire to age well.

Aging well

Aging well may seem paradoxical. Aging will happen to each of us with resultant effects (good and bad) on our bodies and minds. One of the goals we may set for ourselves is to stay mentally sharp through frequent engagement in activities that keep us cognitively fresh and on point. Take your pick of activities, but they should make use of our strong sense of curiosity and require that we intensely focus for a period just on that activity. These types of activities should be *flow* experiences for us and contribute to building and maintaining healthy self-esteem, self-concept, internal locus of control, and self-efficacy.[28]

As we age many people fail to distinguish between older people and assume we are all the same. This is completely socially constructed and bears no resemblance to actual reality. We varied a great deal in our expressions of sensation seeking and sensitivity as younger people and continue to do so now. Each person is quite different in attitude, temperament, and life experiences that contribute to the way we interact with other people and with the world. We need to acknowledge that difference and not fall prey to the human tendency to homogenize groups of people (even groups we are a part of).

One of the issues we may face is a growing sense of pessimism due to prolonged exposure to a society consumed with ego-driven, superficial, marginally empathic individuals. That wearing effect can make it tempting to view life and its many possibilities in a negative light or attribute negative events in our lives solely to ourselves. This makes the issue of self-care even more critical. As I wrote in *Thrive* self-care should be elevated to the level of a spiritual practice for us because without effective consciously chosen strategies to cope with stress keeping our physical, mental, and spiritual selves resilient and strong we cannot hope to access our true potential. That would be a loss for ourselves, our families, and our communities.

Living in community

We began this chapter discussing the socialization process, which we said largely determines how we view the world and imposes on us various group norms and values. We then looked at how that influence even extends to how we experience and express emotions; then we moved to a discussion of the need for emotional regulation emphasizing the need to own our emotions and reactions to them. Next, we unraveled the complexities of gender and gained an appreciation of the not so subtle differences in the way we experience life as males and females acknowledging the narrowness of the socially constructed notion of gender. Gender, as we said, is a flexible construct that will likely continue to be negotiated by each generation. Lastly, we looked at issues of aging and the need to reimagine longevity as an opportunity to continue our journeys of personal growth, reduction of ego, and making and enjoying the connections between people.

This leads us to a prime consideration for this chapter: *sensitive sensation seekers may be extremely valuable, necessary members of our communities if we are able to find the right contexts in which to serve.* Sensory processing sensitivity and sensation seeking evolved as traits that helped facilitate the survival of tribes of early humans in likely difficult times when securing alternative food sources and being aware of predators (animal and human), along with reproductive success, were key to the survival of the tribe.

Remember how we said, in chapter 1, that the greater our range of possible behaviors the greater our ability to perform well in context-specific ways? Both sensation seeking and sensory processing sensitivity increases our range of possible behaviors for our benefit and the benefit of our communities. These evolved psychological mechanisms did not evolve to make our lives miserable; our society does that well enough on its own; instead, these adaptations exist to enhance the survivability of our species. The sensitive sensation seeker being in a sub-group of 15-20% of the population and of that group comprising only 30% must have yielded an evolutionary advantage over time as similar context-specific problems of survival and reproduction presented themselves. It's impossible to know the exact nature of the specific problems of survival or reproduction, but they likely involved problems associated with living in a tribe: living in community.

Today our task is to understand better the ways in which these traits can be best developed and utilized by modern humans to solve some of the problems our society has created like loneliness, fear, anxiety, depression, uncertainty about the worth of life, and distance from community. Sensitive sensation seekers have likely been people who moved from fascination to fascination, were probably not always understood or misunderstood by those around them, and existed as leaders rather than followers, shamans and medicine men than laypeople, and explorers than settlers.

The "Star Trek" gene (as I like to think of sensation seeking) is better suited to exploration, discovery, and breaking a few rules in pursuit of the novel and new than a rote existence requiring less propensity for the above. The sensitive gene is better suited to reflecting, creativity, empathy, and subtleties. The combination of both may seem quite the opposite, yet many highly sensitive people enjoy novelty, find boredom very problematic, and seek out intense experiences (if they can be in control). The sensitive sensation seeker has to find ways to embody both with equal presence and privilege.

I have met everyone from corporate executives to chronic job-hoppers, the spiritual seeker to the rugged individualist, and the extreme thrill seeker to the soft-spoken yet unpredictably intense wild card. All were sensitive sensation seekers and impressed me with their stories of living in community with others who often did not understand them (especially their sensitivity), but sometimes their sensation seeking tendencies.

The real challenge for us all is to consciously choose ways to enact our traits in the world in ways that lift up other people and in so doing lift up ourselves. The sensitive sensation seeker may possess the rare combination of exquisite sensitivity to others, combined with deep reflection and concern overlaid with a twin need to experience the new and novel. What may become of such people? What are the implications for communities that value and respect the deep-thinking and feeling people who are compelled by their genes to explore the new frontiers? These types of questions should be explored by each of us as we pass through this all too brief life.

Key Takeaways

- Socialization is the process by which we learn what it means to be human in our society.
- Society's beliefs, values, and norms are entirely arbitrary and vary greatly from culture to culture.
- We learn which emotions and aspects of personality are socially approved and which are not; leading us

to struggle with rejected parts of ourselves that seek to find expression throughout life.
- Effective emotional regulation for sensitive sensation seekers requires more of a conscious effort than for others.
- Sensitive sensation seekers may prefer non-conforming autonomy and may take social rejection as motivation to continue on our unique life paths.
- Males and females may be more accepted for sensation seeking behaviors than for sensitivity, but sensitivity serves a cautionary function that counterbalances risk-taking.
- An integral masculinity would include traditionally feminine aspects such as cooperation, nurturing, caring, mentoring, and an emotional vulnerability in a way that redefines masculinity as broader-based, yet still "tough."
- Sensation seeking for females may be a gateway through which others may access her sensitive self in time.
- Aging is a social construction. We are entirely free to reinvent ourselves until our last breath!
- Sensitive sensation seekers may hold enormous potential for humanity if we can both master ourselves and direct our energies toward the realization of humankind.

Part 3
Narratives

In the last part of this book, I offer stories from sensitive sensation seekers detailing their experiences of life. The stories are at times visceral and contemplative, wise beyond words, yet indicative of much suffering, and thought provoking in their raw humanness. In as much as I have distilled their interviews down to quotes here I offer their full, unadulterated narratives to allow their voices to be heard full and clear.

When I invited the sensitive sensation seekers in this study to write their own narratives I gave them only the simple request to "write about their lives." I did not wish to steer or influence how, or what they might write about trusting in the creativity and openness they had so graciously provided in participating in the study. What I found in the results often affected me deeply as I felt intimations of my life (as a fellow sensitive sensation seeker) in their lived experiences.

As a researcher, I know the best research usually results from the researcher's passionate interests fueled by curiosity. In this case, the creation of these narratives and subsequent inclusion in this book reminded me of Danny's admonition regarding the value in finding and communing with kindred spirits. I found tremendous personal validation in knowing that my experience of life is not entirely unique, yet also not entirely homogenous. We are each expressions of life shaped and twisted by circumstances and people in an ever-unfolding garden of blooms.

Chapter 9
The Talking Stick

<u>Joshua</u>

When I was still in high school my father bought me a Harley Davidson motorcycle, a small one mind you, but one that became my magic carpet ride to freedom. I was totally surprised. I guess he thought the bike might help my temperament, which was always unpredictable and often volatile. Little did he know at the time that he was actually providing medicine for me to survive his angers, and the chronic tension that pervaded my childhood home. Little did he know that in giving me that bike he was, in fact, launching me into a life of escape and pushing the edge of the envelope as a method of self-preservation. I was far too sensitive for my environment, which has been a pattern that lasted a lifetime.

As a child, I was considered too sensitive by my family. The prevailing question was always "what is wrong with Joshua?" I was jittery, edgy, and seething with an inner rage. My dad liked to say that I was just high strung. Of course, I took that recurring statement as shame, which only made matters worse. Therefore, in my teens, I started a self-destructive pattern that lasted almost my whole life. Of course, as a male, I could not show my feelings or even talk about them to anyone else. So, I rode my motorcycle, often dangerously.

No, as a young man I was supposed to act like I was bullet proof. Unfortunately, I was not, and to make matters worse I lived in a home where I constantly felt under intense pressure to conform to the often angry dictates of a World War II veteran silently suffering from

Thrill

PTSD. With the bike, I could take off, and explore the outside world with impunity, feeling the intoxicating sense of freedom and exploration that relieved the stress. The adrenaline was exhilarating and made me forget my own angers and terrors of my childhood home. Of course, I pushed myself to the limit, because what else would an adolescent male be doing with too much testosterone pumping through his body? Eventually, I had three pretty serious motorcycle wrecks, but that did not seem to deter me, and I never cried.

As I grew older, that motorcycle was not all of my thrill seeking. I always put myself in the way of dangerous and exciting situations. During my life, I have had knives and guns pulled on me several times. I have engaged in fist fights without even knowing why, and I was always combative by nature. I volunteered for hazardous duty and went into the submarine service when I was in the Navy. I volunteered for combat in Vietnam on two different occasions. I was a test subject for NASA and qualified to fly the second seat in an F104. If it was dangerous Joshua would challenge himself to do it.

One time, around midnight, I remember being in Honolulu, getting drunk, and stupidly riding my motorcycle at 120 miles per hour down the freeway toward the submarine base in Pearl Harbor. I sensed something wrong with myself but was still too unaware of what I was doing and why. Still, that was my first warning. Later on, while in my 30s I got so intoxicated that I couldn't hold my bike up in the middle of an intersection. I just dropped it and walked away as if nothing had happened. I was an unadulterated thrill seeker, and although I didn't know it at the time, I was also a highly sensitive person. I always distracted my feelings with adrenaline. How I never got killed or arrested remains a mystery to me even to this day.

The Talking Stick

After the Navy, I always hung out with PTSD survivors of combat in Vietnam. A lot of drinking went on, and there were violent incidents everywhere I went. Once, I had to calm down a friend of mine, who had flown a Cobra helicopter in combat. He had drawn a 45 automatic pistol and was going to kill some innocent guy at a 7-11 store because he didn't like the way the man looked. That was all very exciting to me at the time. Nobody cried in those days either.

Finally, I decided that I wasn't going to live much longer if I didn't modify my behavior. I got beat up pretty seriously and dumped out in someone's yard, where I woke up with a cop poking me in the ribs with his nightstick. As a result, I sobered up and went on a self-awareness journey that has lasted until this very day. I wanted to help others, perhaps to cover up my own pain, and since I was so familiar with trauma and violence, I volunteered for the crisis hotline in Houston, Texas. I also worked in psychiatric hospitals and was called upon many times to handle violent patients. Only after my therapist challenged me on why I was so attracted to violence did I start making any changes.

I found that I had been doing everything for the adrenaline rush. I was actually a traumatized yet highly sensitive person. I felt things deeply, but could not cry out in pain. As part of my healing, I decided to enter graduate school in clinical psychology when I was already 39 years old. I had to find out why I kept doing such challenging things. As a result, I became a psychotherapist.

While in school I realized that I had a knack for counseling. No matter what stories I heard from patients I innately understood what the people were going through. Nothing seemed to rattle me. It was my highly sensitive nature that helped me become an excellent psychotherapist because I could feel my way through almost any situation. I could know what was going on with someone, even without much talking. I had just needed time and education to become aware of my enthusiasm for sitting on a keg of dynamite. I had finally learned how to go within and calm myself down rather than exploding outward. A whole world of sensations opened up to me.

Throughout this process, I have often thought that I took this counseling career as much for my own good than to help others. I desperately needed to know what made me tick. Over the years I learned a lot from my clients too. Mostly I learned that we are all dealing with common issues. I could feel into them by feeling into myself. I finally became aware that in the past it didn't take much to set me off and that I had to nurture myself first, feel my heart, and not react.

This was about the time I also discovered eastern philosophy. I looked around, read a lot, found spiritual teachers, and mentors. I came to realize that the cause of my problem was not with other people but instead lay within my own self. In order to find out what inner peace meant I learned to meditate, dance, do long distance running, take long hot baths, do sweat lodges, and hang out with calmer people. During this process, I found an inner core that was highly sensitive to everything around it. I started feeling my own heart, noticing nature more, enjoying quiet music, moments by the river, and silence.

Before coming to terms with myself, I had taken a post-graduate training in psychodrama, which can be very traumatic. I had picked the one part of psychology that a PTSD and highly sensitive student could readily understand. I was directing psychodrama groups in

The Talking Stick

psychiatric hospitals where my specialty was trauma. Psychodrama is an action-oriented method which required the director (myself) to be on constant edge for even the slightest change of energy within a protagonist or group of people. It actually requires a highly sensitive person to do this kind of work, but it also leads to early burnout, because highly sensitive people cannot take it for too long without destroying themselves. Of course, there were ways for a director to protect himself, but I was such a thrill seeker that I ignored them. Eventually, I just had to quit.

In the end, I discovered ecstatic dance. I could let go of the mental machinery for a couple of hours at a time, get into my body, and eventually end up feeling completely relaxed. I could see my adrenaline addiction from another standpoint. I kept going back for more and more dance. Eventually, I started my own ecstatic dance communities in Austin, Texas; Santa Fe, New Mexico; and Seattle, Washington. I have since observed thousands of people healing themselves through movement. Ecstatic dance essentially saved my life and as a result, I eventually wrote a Ph.D. dissertation on the practice.

In short, I was a highly sensitive person who did not know who he was for most of his life. After what felt like a series of almost disastrous personal train wrecks I finally stopped trying to unconsciously kill myself and learned how to drop down into my feelings without taking actions because of them. I learned how to feel the addiction to adrenaline and to not put myself in harm's way in order cope with life. I finally found peace, even though it had been a steep learning curve. I even learned how to earn a living by just being myself.

Right now, I do my best not to expose myself to the over stimulation of the larger culture. I hang out with other sensitive people who understand me. I limit my interactions with the craziness of our society. I can stay at peace inside myself, feel myself, protect myself, and I am finally no longer at war with my own soul. My crazy earlier life was a teacher in fact, and eventually led me to ever expanding periods of actual joy.

Robyn

Key elements of being both an HSP who scores 27 out of 27 on Elaine's test and very much a sensation seeker have been huge influences on my life. I have had a great many challenges and traumatic experiences throughout my life that have harmed me psychologically and physically, and my response to many of these experiences has been exacerbated by my sensitivity. Arguably, though, for me, aspects of my sensation seeking personality have contributed towards a particular type of resilience associated with resolving and managing these experiences, often turning them into strengths and opportunities after a time.

There are certainly huge tensions that remain between my sensitive self and my sensation seeking components of myself. We are risk takers. I like to think I have mostly taken "managed" risks throughout my life, but I am certain others would not see it that way. Many of these risks have allowed me to explore key parts of myself and the world around me to a much greater degree than would otherwise be possible. I believe that my conscientiousness, in particular, marries really well with my sensation seeking self to create a kind of innovative, dogged determination that many who know me well would say characterizes many aspects of my experience including managing the many traumas that I have experienced.

The Talking Stick

I have worked many years as a counselor and recently in my 40s have upgraded these qualifications to be a mental health clinician/social worker. This study and my work connect closely to both aspects of the trait for me as I much prefer to work on a self-employed basis, enjoying the level of innovation and aspects of risk that are possible in this space.

Being an HSS and HSP allows me to be more intuitive and more authentic, to take chances that are necessary in life to achieve authenticity to the greatest degree possible. When I am empowered, it allows me to be courageous. It very much helps give me the courage, belief in my uniqueness and other things that are necessary to find a way on the path. Sensitivity is often about inward responses to the external world and sadly less about intuitive experiences. My intensity that is core to me combines beautifully with my intuitive self that is allowed to come to the fore a bit more because of my sensation seeking self. When my self-confidence allows this cocktail to manifest, beautiful things normally occur in my life for myself and those around me. This manifestation is also important in my work as I need to keep challenging, keep asking questions as a mental health clinician and researcher and this twin phenomenon of sensation seeking and strategically-led intuition are often guiding lights for me here. But when the balance is not there, it can all go to pot. Understanding the balance within these sometimes competing forces is paramount.

Finally, the following lyrics describe my experience of being a sensation seeking HSP very well ... from The Easy Way by Dar Williams (particularly the listed lyrics although the whole lyrics are also relevant)

Thrill

Cause I never took heavy words for granted
And I never took undeserved advantage
No, I never took the easy way
So why don't you take it a little easy on me now?

Out on the road, I had so many questions
I thought I would explode just for some attention
Like an acolyte, I saw the flames of towering tapers
Almost proselytized by those gleaming piles of paper

Cause we don't want to be the ones
To lie and cheat and slander
So we hold each other up to the higher standard
But I'll tell you what; I'll never try to make it hard
Cause when you're hard just to be hard
The only thing that's hard is you

So here's what I took, I kept the wine and laughter
Until every path just grew up and ever after
Through the peaks and twisty canyons
I made many great companions
Best of all is the one who loves me like you do

Cause I never took heavy words for granted
And it's much too late to even want the shortcut
Yeah, I never took the easy way
So you can take it a little easy on me now
Cause we know that easy's never easy anyhow

Stephanie

I quit school in grade ten. On my 16th birthday, I moved out. I never knew what I wanted to be; I didn't care. I hooked up with a guy I knew from my runaway adventure. We ended up married for nine months. I went back home at 17 with Mom and Dad. My Mom got me a job in a sewing factory. I towed the line well for a while and went to a trade college. It was drafting. Eventually, I ended up getting married again, which didn't work out. Number one was a sensation seeker; number two was a total dud. I've been married three times. None worked out.

Sometimes I think I should try another dating site and sometimes I just wish they'd bring back the good old-fashioned barn dance. These sites are so superficial. I've just decided to leave it up to fate. I just wish somebody would introduce me to somebody. I think it would be so nice to have a partner, but I've gotten so used to doing what I want I don't necessarily want to live with someone again. I'd just like to go on dates.

I was deeply affected by my common-law husband when he used to rag me for needing to lose weight. I just stopped caring at some point and got so fat. His negativity affected me very deeply. After I had left him, I lost 55 pounds in nine months because I had some positive feedback from friends. As soon as I left him, it was so wonderful. I kicked another person to the curb who was a friend and explained to them my reasoning. She responded with an extremely nasty email, which completely confirmed my belief that she was toxic. Since then I've been cleansing. I knew this woman for ten years, and that left me a little bit lonelier. I have other friends all over the country, but no one close. I'd rather lose a false friend though.

I'm expanding my social circle by going to a local Unitarian church that doesn't care what religion you subscribe to. There was a transsexual at a recent meeting, and I knew for sure they were inclusive then! There's something about my gf that makes us high on each other. We have a ball! We've been on four vacations. We don't have to be drunk; we feed off of each other'

Thrill

silliness. There doesn't have to be alcohol involved otherwise I'll just get into trouble.

Boredom is still a problem in my life. I like to wander over to the bars in my town and talk to people, but they don't want to talk back because they are the old boy's network. It's just the guys sitting around. I'm surrounded by pubs, but it's just this old boy's network. Once in a while, they will open up to me with their problems, maybe it's because I'm empathic, but then they're back to their old boy's network the next weekend. It's boring.

Stay out of trouble, don't get hurt! I fell down a flight of stairs at a concert and do not recall the fall. It's one thing to be a high sensation seeker and another just to be plain stupid. I've been plain stupid too much! I was pretty drunk that night. I usually get myself into trouble because of the sensation seeking. It's been a journey of self-awareness all along because I've always been with a partner. Three years later I'm still single. Finally, it feels like I'm me! I'm 56 years old and finally asking who I am.

Nicki

I'm just a human being like everyone else. My levels of sensitivity, overwhelm, boredom or stimulation go up and down depending on my state of mind. The more present I am, the more content and loving I feel. The more I get caught up thinking about how I feel, how I might feel, how other people think of me, what I think about their feelings, the less centered I feel.

I have preferences, dislikes, talents, weaknesses, and fears, but at any given moment, none of those traits needs to define me. The less seriously I take them, the more resilience I find I have, and the more resources, including love, are available to me to deal with whatever comes up. I can enjoy the subtleties my sensitivity allows me to notice and have fun with the crazy things my sensation-seeking leads me into, knowing I'll bounce back and be fine if I overdo anything or get too excited, frustrated, whatever. The more deeply I see this, the more fun I have being me.

Christine

I don't think I've had more sexual partners than others, but I've had a lot of first dates. I guess they can tell; it's going to require more from them, and they aren't interested. I feel I intimidate men. I'm not easy or naïve.

What excites me about the honeymoon period of a relationship is the fun part. The chemistry that attracts two people. I met a man a couple of years ago. He was SO much fun. He enjoyed doing the things I enjoy doing. However, the deal breaker is that he is a smoker. A heavy smoker. I thought I could overcome that aspect because he was so much fun. I found myself very depressed or maybe more introverted when I was around his smoke...such as in the car. Although he was a respectful smoker, it really bothered me, and I could not adjust. He'd spend more time outside...even in the dead of winter or heat of summer...smoking. Not because he was an outdoorsman. He didn't ride a bike or run or camp...or do anything outdoorsmen do. He was outside to smoke and expected me to be out with him. He asked me if I saw a future with him and I told him no. I told him, with everything he had to offer, he takes so much more than he gives. He's narcissistic plus I'm very sensitive to cigarette smoke. It's a deal breaker.

I've never felt the need or desire to experiment with women or multiple partners at once. I do think there's a need for sex toys, especially for a single female who hasn't had a physical relationship in many years like me. In my opinion, a physical relationship changes for men and women as we age. It's not going to be like it was in our youth no matter how many blue pills you take. It's always been easy for me to connect with men and women. I'm a good listener and allow them to talk about themselves. I feel I was much more of a high sensation seeker in my youth than I am now. I'm much more cautious now. Two years ago, I wanted to go skydiving. Now, I don't have the desire. Seems foolish and too dangerous. Scary or suspenseful movies (not torture or bloody) movies have always appealed to me. Mystery appeals to me. Gives me something to figure out (depth of processing). Predictable is boring. I still want to do things that give me an adrenaline rush, as long as it's not too risky. Couldn't do it very often either as its too exhausting. Halloween is my favorite time of the year and anyone who knows me knows that about me. I like haunted houses and dressing up. I've never had a paranormal experience, but it appeals to me because of the mystery behind it.

Shortly after my divorce, I met a really fun guy. I needed fun in my life, and he was exactly what I needed. We dated on and off for about five years. During that time, I learned that he was a mama's boy, and mom would always be #1 in his life...no matter what. Any women he had in his life would be strictly for a physical relationship because mom couldn't provide that. She satisfied all his other needs. The most meaningful relationship I've ever had in my adult life was with a man who treated me like a queen. He raised the bar. He taught me what respect felt like. He lived 4 hours away and had a teenage son, so we saw each other when it was the son's turn to spend the weekend with his mom. Our relationship went full circle in 10 months.

The Talking Stick

The distance would come between us but I also realized (and maybe he did too) that any relationship can be great on a part-time basis, which is basically what we had. I still want to believe that I can find that kind of respect....fulltime. Might be a pipe dream or fairytale. My daddy was an exceptional human being and had the highest respect for women. All women. My ex was nothing like my daddy. He was more like my controlling mother and I felt he would (and did) stand up to her in my defense if necessary. I fell in love with him because of his drive and determination...at such a young age. He was 24 when we met. He displayed anger in a way that was uncommon but familiar, so I didn't see it as a red flag. Although he was never physically abusive, as my mother was, he was verbally and emotionally abusive. I'm deeply wounded by the treatment I received from my mother and my ex BUT...I spend a lot of time in introspection and am overcoming. I'm sure others have done what I've done, but I don't know any. I should be in poor health and some sort of addict. Perhaps even homeless with serious mental health issues. I'm not only overcoming but thriving in a way I never thought possible...for someone with my history.

When I meet men now, they are looking for that fun, outgoing, throw caution to the wind kind of "girl." I'm not that girl anymore. In fact, I'm a woman now. My inner child...the little girl in me...is deeply wounded and I'm very protective of her. I know I have a fun side but I also know when someone is trying to take advantage of that fun side because THEY see it as a sign of weakness. This may sound cliché, but at this point in my life, I need a man to fall in love with my naked soul, not my naked body.

<u>Stacey</u>

Thrill

My childhood was crazy. My Mom had a lot of mental health issues. We found out later she had post-partum depression and never really treated the cause, just took lots of medicines and was misdiagnosed with lots of things. I later found out in my life that I don't have to be like that and don't want to be like that and I've recently dealt with my own issues. My memories of childhood really were daycare, babysitters. My mom always put her social life ahead of us. When she divorced my Dad things became a lot more hectic with taking care of the house and my younger sister. My mom was married four times and my dad four times. We really took care of her. She was on Prozac, Xanax, and alcoholism became pretty prevalent as well. Life just became all about her, similarly for my dad.

When I started learning this past year how growing up has affected me as an adult I learned I have a lot of codependency type issues. Everybody else's needs were put before mine, except for in the workplace. My biggest need is to balance the different aspects. I get bored. I like to go to the gym to stay motivated and there's people around me, but I don't want to talk to anyone. I just want to do what I do. I have my techniques. I've learned things along the way.

I had some pretty major anxiety for a while. I took Zoloft for a very long time and earlier this year I stopped it because I was feeling so much better and when I did that's when all of the things I've been suppressing and probably numbing came to a head and now I realize it's just like alcohol numbs things the medicine was numbing the reason for my anxiety. Now I take Wellbutrin, which helps with some of the same issues, but doesn't have the same effects as Zoloft. I definitely didn't like the numbing experience.

The Talking Stick

The thing that has helped me the most is meditation. Just to have the balance because I will push myself to a point where the sensation seeking takes over completely. I will push and push and push until I'm exhausted. Meditation has helped me keep my mind in check. I try to strike a balance physically and that helps me with all the other stuff. I think I'm still learning how it's affecting me. It's like the story of the cat who will let you pet him five times, but not six. If you do six he'll bite you. It's the same for my sensation seeking because if I go to six it's much harder to come back. I told my husband about this and he said "Oh my God, that's so you!" It's really a push and pull that is challenging. I'm learning how to balance that and I feel a lot less crazy than I used to.

I was having real issues with stress. My body felt like it was reacting more than it should and then I started realizing I had all of these other things other people didn't have like sensitivities to noise. Certain noises, light (lack of light), things that come up and I wonder why does this bother me?

With the sensation seeking I prefer for things to be different every day. I shifted around a lot in jobs because I get bored easy. I am looking for a job right now and think back to other jobs I've had and what I liked and didn't like. This last year I got a license in real estate and got into it and really didn't like being around weird people out there buying houses. There's some crazy people out there so that didn't last very long. It's kind of become a joke. It's like my husband will say "Okay, what's next?" I would be happy if I could just job hop the rest of my life, but it doesn't look good on a resume and it doesn't allow you to build up your experience. The longest I've stayed at a job is maybe 3 years.

Thrill

Once I learn the rules and processes I start to see applying the same things, not needing the creativity maybe, and I never thought I was creative. I realize now though that the more creativity I have and the more problem solving the better. For whatever reason I thought I was very detailed and enjoyed administrative tasks. As soon as I see it's the same I have to mix it all up. I can't stand to do the same process every time. That's make it much harder for a more structured type of scenario.

At one time I ran a women's health center. It was tough, but I was able to put a lot of creativity into it. That was fun although I didn't make much money. I'm thinking about going into the health and wellness field. My background now is in HR. That field has become much more about compliance and rules and I find myself in the same situation again. It takes the fun out of it. I like the people aspect and the creativity where you're trying to make people happy. Once that's gone and you're just looking at rules and processes that's where I lose interest. It's never a performance issue: I'll do it until I burn out then I'm just done. It's like I have to do something today. It's like a total intolerance.

I like the team environment the best. I was at the top of the team in my HR job and then no one wants to talk to you because you're the company police. That was really hard and I know I will never do that again. Working at home might be good, but I'm really apprehensive. It's hard to give 100% in just a couple of hours here and there. Most of what I do is technology based, but without the human element in it so it just doesn't have the same joy. I was in one job where I was in the field 50% of the time and in the office the other 50%. I think that's probably the best scenario for me. I'm really not good being micromanaged or dealing with people who won't just tell you what to do and let you do it.

The Talking Stick

I do like having a manager set the parameters and guidelines so I know where my limits are. I know what I need to do and how to accomplish my goals. I think I have a very idealistic view out of what I want from a job.

I'm not a physical risk taker. I'm always aware of potentially getting injured. If the adrenaline starts rushing I'm not as comfortable. The anxiety feeling comes on when the adrenaline rushes. Recently my friend took me to do indoor skydiving and I literally thought I was going to have a meltdown right there. On the flipside if it comes to work I will take a risk to jump into a new business. I wasn't afraid. I was definitely in the mindset of I'm going to try this because if I don't I'm going to regret it. A lot of those kind of things: the more mental risks I'm not afraid to try. I always get a little anxious, but it's worth it in the end.

People have told me I need to go into interior decorating or house staging. They always say my house feels so comfortable. It's always done so artistically. I never really paid attention to it I just did it. I've never thought of it as a strength, but I definitely have a way of visualizing how I want things to be. I'm always more concerned with the visual layout of things, even forms. I really like to have a problem and think of what's a new, efficient, creative way to do it. That's more where my creativity came out. I think I thought I was someone else then I realized I was working really hard to be who I thought I was and I can just let that stuff go and be who I am: it's a lot easier.

The biggest thing with sensation seeking for me is feeling bored and not liking consistency, but needing consistency to not feel overwhelmed. I think it means there's this very small area on the spectrum where I'm comfortable. I can go away from that small area for very

Thrill

short times. I'm most comfortable in something that is exciting and new, but maybe with some things I'm comfortable and familiar with. *Probably the need for constant balance is something I feel like I strive for and need more than anyone else around me.* I don't feel like anyone else is having that challenge. I have a friend who is a highly sensitive person, but not a sensation seeker and she just thinks I'm crazy. We do things and I push her to have fun, but know when to stop. She takes me in small bursts. Not too much at a time. It takes other sensitive people to understand us.

It's awesome to finally feel like "Okay, there's other people out there like me, I'm not in this weird bubble!" My addiction is trying to better understand myself and the world. If you're going to have an addiction that's one of the better ones to have. It can only be good.

Meg

I always say I was born in my family storm. My family had three daughters then took in my cousin. He was a year older than me and there was a lot of anger. It was nature versus nurture. The whole focus was on getting him better. I was just in the background and hid from the anger. I was shy, but I did well in school. I never got any acknowledgement though so kind of gave up in the fourth grade.

I was always told I couldn't do things because I was short in stature. I started drinking when I was 12 and smoking pot the next year and acid the next year. I always got unwanted attention from men. In my senior year of high school I ended up meeting this guy and thought how brilliant he was. He was actually jealous and a narcissist. I lived vicariously through him, supporting him in everything he wanted to do in life. He became a firefighter/paramedic and I was just like "Oh my Gosh!" I enjoyed him being gone for 24-48 hours at a time, but when he came home I wanted to hear about his adventures and drama he went through. I really did live through him for my sensation seeking.

He ended up on disability in chronic pain and for many years I became a prisoner to that pain and sought ways to get out of that. I had this welding shop to do artwork, but that stopped working for me at some point. I decided to make soap and renovated my shop, sold my equipment and spent lots of time learning how to make soap. That was a pretty intense part of my life.

We ended up losing our home. He was retired and never allowed me to work so I was pretty stuck. I saw that as an adventure. I wanted to get out of the house. He saw it as a tragedy. It was kind of a thrill to lose my home because I felt really good about it. I wanted to get out because I knew it meant something else was happening. We ended up separating a couple of years later and immediately I went to Mexico. He led me to believe I did not get any of his pension, so I just lived on like $500 a month, but I was still traveling between family members. I was enjoying it being in a foreign country, not knowing the language and getting out of my element.

It's been three years ago, and I've been traveling ever since. Once I was getting a fair share of the pension, I saved up, and that's when I went on that couch surfing trip in the UK for two months. Nothing feels like home so I went back to Arizona and stayed for a bit, but realized I couldn't stay so I put out my interests and ended up in Hawaii so now I'm here! For a while, it was just surviving for a few weeks at a time. Next month I'm going to another place not knowing how long I'll be there. It's a thrill; it's an adventure!

Thrill

My biggest concern is finding time to be alone knowing that it's a house with other people. I was kind of worried about that. For quite a few years I just isolated myself. I have a storage unit, a backpack and a carry on. Those are my worldly possessions and at my age starting over I'm okay with it. I just totally renovated my life. I'm considering working on another farm because it's away from everybody else and there's nothing back here but the jungle, very private. I work in the garden so it's very quiet and I can just work alone. I really like working alone, but I do like one on one time with others.

I gave up the notion that I'm going to help anyone. I don't have to worry about helping anyone. People that are willing to look at the deeper meaning in life are the ones I connect with. The ones who connect with spirituality or self-discovery. I'd rather be around those people.

I always have to seek out something: knowledge, projects or something. If I'm not involved in something, I just sleep. I can sleep for long periods of time. I prefer to have multiple projects going on at once. I'm very interested in learning how to make new things like the foods here. Learning new foods and experiencing new foods. I cook a lot too.

Feeling safe and wanting to understand the world seems to be more important to me than sensation seeking. In the past couple of years, I've found a new need for self-care. I've always known that thoughts are things, but I never thought my thoughts mattered. It's like I didn't equate them to any form of life, which is the place to be in a narcissistic relationship. But, that's when a lot of our problems started: when I started taking care of myself. The people who just keep telling me "No, you can't do that!" I just stopped listening to them. I'm really starting to believe my own beliefs are my own reality. If people aren't resonating with that I have no need to talk to them. I'm taking care of myself now.

I'm thinking I might stay here. I would like to be a part of some retreat and take care of the land. Nurture myself and hopefully be an example for my kids. That's kind of where I'm at. I'm 56 and maybe should be thinking of some kind of normal life. My new normal is walking around barefoot all the time and playing in the dirt. It suits me. This girl I know, we're renting a van and just taking off. We don't know what we're going to do, so I guess it's just a sensation seeking adventure.

I have a blog now. For my whole entire life, no one ever heard what I have to say. Now in group discussions, I can say something, and nobody hears me. I've always been hiding and not having a voice. That's what I'm working on. I'd like to be a public speaker, even though others do not hear my voice.

I see possibilities here where I can help someone build something if not myself. It's really important for us to disconnect from everything and then reconnect. It would be an anti-5 star resort; that's what I'm calling it, where people could get away and reconnect to the Earth. That's my role: creating sacred spaces.

There're so many people who are still feeling so wounded. They don't have to claim that. I could always see things in a different way. Just to trust that is probably the truth. I imagine I'm a river and absorb the energy and just see it flowing out of me. I've never thought of myself as a leader. I think maybe the high sensation seekers are going to be the ones who start standing up and start being more visible and championing others who maybe aren't so bold and daring.

Danny

Thrill

There's a sticker on my motorcycle helmet that says "If you're not on the edge, you're taking up too much room." My life has been one of extremes.

My mom had a way of marrying child sadists, and she offered her children up to them as if to gods. My earliest memory is of my father punching me in the face. Her second husband was sick and twisted, yet he could manipulate subtle energy. Sometimes when he was in a good mood we'd gather around for a show of his powers. He'd do dousing or lay hands on people's wounds or predict where neighborhood runaways were hiding out. Once he hypnotized my sister's fourteen year old friend and I saw her "turn into a board." With nothing but her head on one chair and her heals on another he sat on her with all his weight while she lay flat, his eyes all trance-like and crazy. Once he hypnotized me and to my own surprise I went under deeply, and strangely, he appeared to me as the devil, which was horrifying and surreal. Finally he snapped me back to normal, but I've been a little haunted by that ever since. Living with him I was hyper-vigilant to his meanness, but beyond that to some liminal realm he seemed to inhabit that never quite touched ground; always in subtle spheres of the paranormal. I always had to watch his face to predict his behavior.

As I got older I began to read faces like tea leaves. I had a strange talent for knowing where people are from. Just as people from different regions have different vocal accents, I could see their facial accents as well. For instance, when I'm at a hot springs retreat up north with lots of other people from the Bay area, I can tell whether people are from SF, Oakland, Berkeley, or the North Bay. I can also often tell what people do for a living, or even more personal things by their faces.

The Talking Stick

Since my mom's husband didn't work we lived in a ghetto on welfare. In junior high a bus took kids from my neighborhood to a nice school across town. I was a white kid bused into a black school for racial integration. I was neglected and hungry, slept in a little shed in my back yard with my dog, so sometimes had fleas on me, and my shoes were held together with duct tape. I was also subjected to capricious felonies on my body and mind at home. Tough times for a sensitive kid.

In high school I was relieved to be back in my own neighborhood. These days it's common for middle class white kids to appropriate black culture, but in the seventies it was rare, and I came into it organically as a native. I was a deejay for the school's low watt soul radio station, and was dating a black girl. I was reading all these urban coming of age books, like Manchild In The Promised Land, and Soul On Ice, and saw my life through that romantic prism. It was typical teenage identity experimentation but driven to extremes by my HSS and HSP sensibilities.

One night when I was fifteen I was watching television and a girl came on the show and I instantly fell madly in love in some inexplicable way I'd never felt before. Six months later I was working at a grocery store and saw that a movie was being made at the gas station on the same lot, so I walked over and introduced myself to the beautiful blond star. Shortly into the conversation I realized it was the same girl I'd fallen in love with on television. We were immediately drawn to each other and hung out the whole three weeks they were there filming, and I even got a little part in the film. I was so infatuated, one night I was in her dressing room watching her get make up, and fell under the spell of her beauty like a rabbit immobilized by a snake. I literally couldn't take my

Thrill

eyes off her for a half hour, and went home that night embarrassed to think about it. That short period of trance was a microcosm of the spell I was under the whole time she was in town. After she left I got really depressed. I think it's common for HSP's and/or survivors of child abuse to do fairly well until a life crisis occurs, then to just spiral. So began my long dark night of the soul.

I just lost my way and became antisocial and started fighting all the time at school, finally getting expelled early in my junior year. Home had become unbearable so I left and ended up joining the army. One drill sergeant always had it in for me and one day I found him drunk, beating up my friend. I pulled him off and punched him, for which he got me discharged, and I found myself barely seventeen and homeless. I was too messed up for anyone to employ and often had to steal to survive. Half desiring to die, I'd shoot drugs, passing the needle around whole rooms of junkies. This was the early eighties, only months before AIDS hit, but I dodged that bullet. I'd sleep in cars or all night movies. I'd gone voluntarily mute, having descended leagues into myself and my circumstances without even the consolation of knowing I'd survive.

At the depths of this loss I'd hear Bruce Springsteen's song, Darkness on the Edge of Town. He sang like a trapped animal swearing to rise above it. To quote Pete Townsend, "When Springsteen sings, that's fuckin' triumph, man." As an HSS/HSP I can be deeply moved by poetry or the spirit of a song, and this spoke to some primal hope in me. I took a few speech classes at a junior college, and found some latent spirit inside. I started to dream of rising above that life. I got a tattoo of a bird on my chest and fantasized about flying one day. I was sleeping in my car, but one night I drove out to the San Francisco suburbs and looked at the beautiful houses, imagining the happy families inside, and someday

The Talking Stick

living in one myself. But a cop pulled me over and asked what I was doing there. He said my Nova looked like a getaway car and the residents had complained.

After 'wandering in the desert' for seven years I finally got a good plumbing job. But, like many HSP's, I didn't like working for other people; the hierarchy, the looking over my shoulder. After three years my anxiety began to spill out and I got fired, and swore I'd never work for anyone else again. I was tired of trying to fit into the world and decided to make my world fit me, so I started my own arbor care company. This was an incredible relief, and satisfying in so many ways. I loved the animal sense of not knowing whether I'd kill or die when I woke up every day. It makes life exciting and seems so much more natural than punching a clock. I saved my money and one day I drove out to those suburbs and bought one of those houses.

I married a great woman and finally settled down enough to pursue my longtime dream of flying. Hang gliding became my life. I've read that all fears are ultimately a fear of death. There's a moment when you're launching your glider off the edge of a cliff; it's a huge wing and the terrain is often rough. The wingtips and nose have to be at the perfect angle. This is the most dangerous moment and any misstep and you'll tumble off the mountain. You begin to run, eyes on the horizon, the nose, the wingtips and the ground all at once. You hold the control bars lightly, not with a death grip, and you realize this is your whole life between your thumb and your forefingers. All those interminable fears blow behind you in the rush of wind. There's only death and life now; every motion decides which, all in this cup of time. You're the author, the master; you own life. Your feet get lighter and you exit the planet.

Thrill

Once, in the early days of the sport, a reporter asked a pilot if hang gliding was just an escape from reality. "Totally," he said, sidestepping the implication that people have some moral obligation to lead boring lives, and that smiling in the face of death is irresponsible. I think trying to live lives sanitized of death causes death to seep into its marrow, demanding to be recognized. That's why Buddhists say "think daily of death." When I'm burdened by cares in the morning and I climb a redwood tree for my job the thought occurs to me that I may die, and that possibility is a window for my cares to fly from, and I feel more alive.

I was drawn to extreme cultures, something that stretched me to the edges of my intensity. I was in a religious family for a couple years, a college scholar, a Dead Head, and I hung with the Oakland Hells Angels for a while. Riding with them felt like marching in to liberate Paris, people just seemed to stand back and salute. I'd been around some other clubs, but these guys had a mystique that guys in other clubs lacked. Sonny Barger, their old president used to say, "We don't recruit, we recognize." I knew what he meant. They were actually really sensitive, I thought, beneath it all. One night we caught a bunch of locals messing with our bikes and we chased them for several blocks and caught them, but let them go with a warning. I'll never forget that moment with those guys, the spirit in the dark streets that night, feeling like a brother, pimpin' home through the valley of the shadow of death.

I continued in my adventures and at one point realized I'd flown hang gliders, airplanes, sailplanes, skydived, scuba-dived, bungee jumped, surfed, kite boarded, white water rafted, kayaked, dirt biked and done trapeze arts, but was bored with life. It seemed I was banging my head against the edge of the universe, and one

The Talking Stick

day I heard a knock from the other side. I saw a documentary on near death experiences, and could see in the interviewee's faces that they'd truly been to the spirit world. I was absolutely fascinated by their stories, and later by personal readings from the world's best psychic mediums. Talking to the dead is a head turning experience. I'd always been skeptical about life after death, but was finding convincing evidence for it, the implications of which were staggering for this life. Brother can you par-a-digm? Life itself became interesting, and I rarely did thrill sports anymore.

    I gave up drugs and alcohol and became committed to finding some kind of confidence in myself again. I found a couple of support groups for survivors of child abuse, and made a few friends I could finally talk about it with. I was spending a lot of time with them. Elaine Aron wrote that there may come a time when an HSP realizes his partner isn't an HSP, and how difficult that may be. After many years of marriage, raising three beautiful kids, I found myself growing further and further from my wife, and sadly we decided we were better friends than soul mates. I was interested in alchemy, and shadow work. There was one survivor friend with whom I could share all the pain and shame I'd felt I had to keep hidden all my life. Childhood trauma survivors are one of the HSP 'subcultures,' and this was my first experience of the level of depth I could have with another HSP. I wrote a poem about it, which is at the bottom of this narrative.

    Meanwhile I continued to search out evidence for life after death, and whatever energy it is that people call "God." I came to see the interconnectedness of everything, and that there are no coincidences. I thought back to how the girl on tv I'd had such a surreal attraction to had magically shown up in my life; all the synchronicity

Thrill

involved for her to be chosen for that role, then for the company to inexplicably decide to film the movie four hundred miles from Hollywood, right on the lot where I worked. It was a sign to me that despite the holocaust in my soul after she left, there was divine consciousness involved in starting me on my deeper journey through that loss. And it spoke to the power of attraction kindred spirits have; that we were destined to meet due to some psychic proximity that superseded physical geography and circumstance.

There had always been a certain type of person that would completely disarm me with a single glance. I'd run into them very rarely but when I did I instantly felt profound well-being. A few years ago I discovered personality typing and realized there was actual science to this phenomenon, and most the people I'd reacted to that way were INFP's on the Meyers Briggs system, or fours on the enneagram, and all of them were HSP's. I'd searched for myself in so many places, and they all seemed to take more of me than I received. Most the people I meet are opaque rather than translucent; vaguely flat rather than mysteriously intense; mundane, rather than ethereal; one dimensional, rather than beautifully layered. I go through my days measuring the distance from people rather than sensing any meaningful encounter. I used to fill these gaps with self judgement and blame, but have come to understand myself and others in a new way.

I realized HSP's have a different emotional disposition; we speak a different emotional language; we literally vibrate on a different frequency, and as such we feel alienated from the world, yet we have an equal and opposite reaction with other HSP's. When I saw how good I could feel with kindred spirits I made it my life's purpose to surround myself with them. I found meet ups for sensitives, and we'd all be blown away by what we called

The Talking Stick

"the vibe," when we were together; it was like some kind of emotional levitation. This warm suffusion powerfully permeated the atmosphere in a way no one had ever experienced before in this specifically selected group of people. It was as if we'd made some breakthrough in a hitherto unnoticed realm of social/emotional science. Interestingly, if a non-HSP were to enter the circle the whole vibe would fall flat.

This was all very validating for my sense of who I am in the world. I realized I wasn't defective, but had some rare gift that could only be accessed by others with the same gift. I let up on myself for not feeling it with most people, knowing that there are some who understand me well. I don't mean to imply that life is easy now, because it's not. I'm an HSP - it feels like I don't exist properly. I chafe against the universe like it's a womb without water. But sharing that with others who feel the same way makes it a lot easier.

Three years ago I saw an online ad for an HSP support group. There was a picture of the facilitator on the page, her face all soft with wonder and philosophical curiosity. Love at first sight can happen with a picture too, I realized. I called her and was further drawn in to her gentle depths. I went to her meeting, and she later told me I was looking right into her, seeing her in a way she'd always wanted to be seen. We began seeing each other and it's been amazing. We intend to start a family soon.

Two Survivors

She threw back the gates of her isolation
and absorbed me
beneath the ages
of earth in her face
to the buried city

Thrill
where children had played

We spoke of the fall
God and rain falling from the sky
father's falling boot steps toward the room
blood and angels on the floor
we were ghosts, and ghosts of ghosts
when they were through

Carrying more than we wanted
and less than we needed
in the diaspora of innocents
to the fallen world

We gathered new countries around us
of carnival mirror souls
who reflected, not beauty
but recognition

"Does it ever come back to you?" she asked
I said, "It's like being on a train
and looking through the window
to the next train
and seeing yourself
and he looks back
but the car slowly pulls away
and you watch yourself go."

As we talked, I thought of Helen Keller
raging in her inarticulation
And how those first words
must have felt like being born

And I wondered if Helen
ever met another like herself
with neither sight nor sound

And what secret language

they must have whispered

into each other's hands.

Jacquelyn Strickland, LPC

Overstimulation. Understimulation. High Sensation Seeking. Optimal Level of Stimulation. Where IS that elusive "optimal level of stimulation" for we HSPs, and how do we cultivate it?

To me it's similar to that sweet spot on a tennis racket – a spot I could rarely find during my short tennis playing days. Or even better, the optimal level of stimulation is like the perfectly tuned guitar or violin. When in perfect tune, the resulting sound is beautiful as the chords and strings become harmonious and generally pleasing.

As a young child I was sorely understimulated. In retrospect, I was extremely bored with little to no access to any kind of enrichment opportunities. I remember holding back tears of disappointment as my single parent mother, who worked two jobs, gently explained to me that piano lessons, dance lessons, Camp Fire girls, or summer vacations all cost money—money that we didn't have.

Luckily I had a great imagination. I filled long summer days with my own unique "high sensation seeking "experiences. I rode Trigger, my imaginary golden palomino horse around the neighborhood. He expanded my small world at the age of 10, galloping about to special places that only we knew about. We would arrive, breathless, each stopping to catch our breath and proud of how fast we could run. Then for the next several minutes we would experience a grand "sense of place" – a place of being happy and content – a feeling of well-being.

Thrill

This was not only time or place I sought after this elusive sense of well-being. Climbing high into my mimosa tree I would sit in the seat formed by three pronged branches that fit my small body perfectly. Tickling my face with the soft, pink blossoms took me into a meditative state where, in retrospect, I know I was communing with God. The God I was blessed to know was loving, kind, and all knowing. I sought this numinous, "god beckoning" experience often. As Elaine Aron has shared in her Comfort Zone newsletter, this numinous state "stirs us, creates a particular emotional state, which can be interpreted as God. We can be swept into a trance, an ecstasy, or reduced to a silent prayer or a deep peace." It was in my beloved mimosa tree that I felt what Elaine calls a "deep, sweet, tranquility, a security and a knowingness." And as she shared: "It may last quite a while--"forever" would be the goal for most who have had the experience. But usually it fades back into the every-day, nonreligious mood."

I longed for this feeling, this spiritual experience to last forever. It has not been surprising that throughout my life I have been blessed by many similar experiences of being transcended into a state of silent prayer, deep gratitude, or overcome with visions that seemed to appear and be meant especially for me. I usually have the experiences in nature. In fact, it was a nature experience sometime around 1999 or 2000 while hiking in Rocky Mountain National park when the "vision" of a HSP Gathering Retreat came to me. Each time these visions appear to me I am usually overcome with soft tears, and brought back to those early days in my mimosa tree.

As an Extrovert HSP, these spiritual experiences are definitely of the high sensation seeking type, I still long for them, although I know the circumstances have to be just right to experience them: solitude in nature where all my senses: sight, sound, smell, become gently stimulated.

The Talking Stick

My intuition then goes into overdrive and I relish the often overwhelming sense of peace – ironically how this sense of peace satisfies a large part of my high sensation seeking temperament.

I credit my dear, sweet, non-HSP mother for teaching me the value of a spiritual life. Her unconditional love understood, honored and witnessed my sensitivity, even though she didn't know how to comfort my bouts of existential depression. I also credit her for making my high school years a bit more bearable. I found high school painfully overstimulating and boring, and I am grateful my Mama listened to my pleas to stay home at least once a month to rest and recover.

Moving to San Francisco in 1973 turned out to be the perfect environment for my HSP Extravert, HSS self. I had a lovely Victorian apartment near Golden Gate Park which offered me comfort, solace and simple, unique beauty. Outside my door was a fascinating world of culture which beckoned me to come alive each day. Sometimes this would take the form of exploring the city on foot, swimming in the ocean, attending impromptu concerts in Golden Gate Park with the likes of Jesse Colin Young, and Grace Slick of the Jefferson Airplane. The totally accepting culture of San Francisco in the 1970s' gifted me with my ideal level of optimal stimulation – seeking stimulation then retreating, seeking it again and again always sure to find novelty, varied and often intense experiences.

As an HSP, I was always cautious about what kinds of intense experiences I would participate in. For example, I declined taking LSD on a beach with a group of people I barely knew. Instead, I became an attentive observer. I freely admit some of the intense experiences I did participate in have provided me with wonderful, lasting memories. For example, it was thrilling to go to my

Thrill

favorite nude beach down on Hwy 1, just South of San Francisco. I remember unabashedly doing handstands in celebration to the three whales that were sighted about 50 yards off short. I will always be eternally grateful for my unique time in San Francisco, as I have never been able to find that particular kind of niche again.

So, my high sensation seeking experiences have never been the thrill seeking kind of sky diving, rock climbing, or river rafting. These particular activities have been a favorite of my older son, who is an Introvert HSP, HSS. It is interesting as I am now in my 6th decade and I am still in search of spiritual experiences, novelty, and intense learning experiences. I think this is one of the main reasons I continue with my beloved HSP Gathering Retreats: they provide novelty, varied experiences, adventure in different places, and a bit of "predictable" risk – as I never know who will show up or how they will turn out. It's an unknown risk – emotionally, intellectually and financially. And it is a risk I am grateful to be able to continue.

With awareness of my needs, for both rest, recovery, this HSP Extravert will continue to seek that often elusive "optimal level of stimulation" through novelty and varied, intense experiences. And if history serves me correctly, I will continue to benefit from allowing this into my life.

Note: *Jacquelyn Strickland, LPC is the co-founder with Dr. Elaine Aron of the HSP Gathering Retreats which began in 2001. Since September of 2016 there have been 32 HSP Gatherings in around the US, in Canada, and Europe.*

Chloe

I first became aware of the concept of high sensation seeking a couple of years ago and immediately began to reflect back on the myriad of ways this trait has impacted my life:

The Talking Stick

At age 9, browsing in one of the most sacred places; the library. Excitement building as I contemplated which literacy adventure I would choose, I came across a massive tome - 'Gone with the Wind.' One thousand and thirty-seven pages of Civil War drama and angst, Mr. Butler, I was swept away. Imagine my chagrin when the well-meaning librarian asked if the book was too advanced for a child my age - challenge accepted! And, a small amount of personal satisfaction when two weeks later I returned triumphant, having read the whole thing.

Fast forward to age 12, when my father and I climbed Mt. Katahdin, the highest mountain in Maine. Standing at the summit looking over the 'Knife's Edge' I experienced so many sensations. The wind whipping in my hair, the seemingly unending horizon of the Atlantic Ocean and the vantage point overlooking four states simultaneously. The dull ache of muscles and pounding heart telling the tale of my ascent over roots and jagged rocks. The pride in my accomplishment.

How I worked for 13 years at a nonprofit organization, starting part time and eventually was promoted to the position of Vice President. Only one year after that promotion, I decided to pack up everything and move 900 miles away to Texas to begin a new career as a landscape designer. No family, no friends, hadn't even met the supervisor I was going to work for. No one understood why, but the timing felt right for a new adventure.

Ironically, or perhaps not, many of the people I consider 'my tribe' also identify as high sensation seekers - we love intellectual challenges, risk, physical challenges, asking the most deep philosophical questions, the newness of experiences and pushing ourselves to be disinhibited or vulnerable. We seem to flock together, as we understand why this calls us. We also understand

Thrill

what it means to be highly sensitive people and the duality both traits (HSP-HSS) bring to our lives. The constant struggle with taking so much on until we are overstimulated and exhausted, yet at the very same time a part of us is completely energized.

Finding balance between the two will undoubtedly be one of my greatest life lessons.

Conclusion

In attempting to distill the vast experiences detailed in this book into concise, meaningful points of discussion I can offer to you I realized that there are a few broad points that seem to cut through the rich complexities of our lives as sensitive sensation seekers. First, is the "pushing through fear" that Jessica mentioned as her vision of the utility of sensation seeking as a trait. Sensitivity is a personality trait that evolved in ancient times as an adaptation to the environment where pausing to check (or withdrawal to gather more information and reflect) proved to be an advantage on average for our species.

Quick emotions, more elaborate processing of stimulation in the brain, and well-thought out actions were, and still are, a survival and reproductive advantage. But when the tendency to withdraw or pause to check is too strong (as might be true for many sensitive people from chaotic, abusive, or neglectful backgrounds) the fear and anxiety may be paralyzing. Paralysis is crippling to well-functioning and ultimately defeating to the purposes of survival and reproduction. Sensation seeking, as a trait that operates on varied, novel, and intense sensation seeking may serve as that "wild friend" who always wants to do something that pulls us out of our comfort zone into experiences we might never have on our own. To have this extra boost embedded within our psyches as highly sensitive people can be a real advantage that enhances our experience of life. The pushing through fear aspect represents a powerful advantage for sensitive sensation seekers over the purely highly sensitive person.

Thrill

Commensurately our ability to push through fear may serve as an example for others to follow who may need the example to follow. If we are in leadership roles our example of "pushing through fear" may be a powerful motivator for others of courage and sheer chutzpah. That same sense of bravado leads me to my second point: being a sensitive sensation may make finding meaningful ways of engaging in the world quite difficult given that we are very susceptible to boredom, may be less apt to conform or follow conventional pathways, and may not be understood by others or at best misunderstood. Our sense of being "different" may be profoundly stamped on how we view ourselves, which can translate in to how we "show up" in the world. We sensitive sensation seekers seem to be an embodiment of Dabrowski's ideal of "marching to a different drummer."

Within this non-conforming, non-conventional paradigm we may indeed be on Dabrowski's path toward advanced personality development, but we may also fall prey to our own natures to seek pleasure and underestimate risk. Taking undue legal, financial, and personal risks can leave our lives in disarray and completely overwhelm the sensitive part of ourselves. The danger is real and we must be vigilant about the risks we take, while caring for the "sensitive friend" inside each of us. The sensitive side is, after all, as open to new experiences as the sensation seeking side, as creative and interested in the new and novel, it just doesn't want to be overwhelmed by poor planning or lack of forethought. We highly sensitive people are deeply conscientious people with a strong need to do everything in our lives well. When we hastily rush into anything our sense of conscientiousness is offended and demands to be heard. Many times though we find that we have a "tiger by the tail!"

Conclusion

The good news is it's entirely possible to find workable balances between both traits. It may require a good degree of life experience, making numerous mistakes along the way and completely overwhelming the sensitive side at times, but when that balance is struck and maintained and we are able to find worthwhile projects to focus our talents and abilities on we may be truly exceptional individuals. The "tiger by the tail" dichotomy may be more real than most of us are willing to admit to ourselves as we present alternately what may be perceived as extraverted energy (outgoing, gregarious, and novelty seeking) or introverted energy (thoughtful, quieter, and introspective).

In most western societies that emphasize productivity, competition, and aggression sensitivity (and those who express empathy, compassion, and a deep, reflective nature) is often pushed aside in the haste to make a profit and increase the bottom line. The task for us as sensitive sensation seekers is to disavow that mindset, assuming along the way all the hardships and risks entailed in non-conforming and being unconventional, and seek out more personally authentic means of engaging our capacities.

I'm not a purist regarding career. I do not advocate for an all-or-nothing approach to finding the "right work." Many of us are quite limited by numerous factors like geography, access to opportunities, and pushing through the fear that accompanies being misunderstood and unconventional (not to mention education, culture, and systemic factors like ageism, sexism, and racism). In fact, many of us *may* do quite well in careers that provide us with a significant degree of engagement in reasonably conventional capacities. Let's not forget that work is not the end all and be all of life. We should also seek engagement and fulfillment beyond the work environment through other activities where we have much more control over the type, level, and duration of stimulation.

As we pass through mid-life we may realize that our bonds to society (obligations to raising our children, holding stable jobs, etc.) are loosened and we sense a new opportunity for reinvention and redefining our identities. What we should perhaps not lose sight of is the real opportunity this time of relative freedom (for many) provides in reconciling our authentic selves, working through previous hurts and failures, and defining for ourselves (and by extension our children and grandchildren) the kind of world we wish to leave behind. Though this may sound high-minded and idealistic my cumulative experiences with sensitive sensation seekers leads me to feel that there is tremendous potential inherent in embodying both sensation seeking and sensory processing sensitivity. Our world (and communities) need visionary leadership, fully realized human beings who can conceive of and enact considerate, inclusive re-visioning of cultural components that affect all of our children and grandchildren.

We, the segment of the species gifted with deep introspection, reflectivity, intuition, and innately creative dispositions, should be the ones tasked with finding and opening the new frontiers. We should be the ones who push ahead when others lack the imagination, inquisitiveness, or intrapsychic energies to craft new models that render old models obsolete. We sensitive sensation seekers should be the ones who become not only the visionary, creative leaders, but also the spiritual seekers who craft a new morality and set of ethics that includes everyone in being "lifted up" to higher levels of consciousness and action in the world.

Conclusion

For those of us who will never make it to the fullest realizations of ourselves the path is still rich, full, and laden with opportunities for consciousness raising and fulfillment. That may require major adjustments to our lives, our perceptions, and our relationships, but the beauty of life lies in its plasticity. Reinventing ourselves on a more or less near-constant basis, as may be the disposition many sensitive sensation seekers identify most closely with and feel oddly constrained by, in a world that seems to value conformity, groupthink, and rote adherence to entirely arbitrary modes of life may not be optional for many of us.

Reinvention, including the dissolution of lower forms, often leads us to higher levels comprising more sophisticated embodiments of creative functioning that mimic the nature of life itself as an ever-unfolding group of systems and processes dedicated to populating and perpetuating myriads of life forms on this fragile planet in the vast ocean of space and time.

About the Author

Tracy Cooper, Ph.D. is a fellow sensitive sensation seeker who holds a doctorate of philosophy in integral studies from the California Institute of Integral Studies. He appeared in the documentary film *Sensitive – The Untold Story* and is the author of *Thrive: The Highly Sensitive Person and Career*. His website may be found at www.drtracycooper.com where he provides consulting services for HSPs in career transition or crisis and for the sensitive sensation seeker. Cooper lives in the Springfield, Missouri metro area with his wife, Lisa, and son, Ben.

ACE's, 28, 29, 30, 33, 51
Adaptations, 4, 20
aging, 28, 185, 186, 189
ancestralization, 6
Attachment style, 93
Behavior, 1, 23, 103
boredom, 12, 13, 14, 20, 35, 36, 41, 46, 60, 62, 63, 64, 65, 66, 67, 73, 74, 78, 81, 84, 88, 90, 99, 101, 106, 108, 136, 139, 142, 168, 175, 179, 185, 191, 203, 231
boundaries, 33, 36, 50, 75, 76, 95, 100, 102, 109, 110, 113, 115, 116, 117, 132
brain, 15, 17, 21, 23, 27, 28, 29, 57, 59, 103, 105, 124, 141, 142, 155, 166, 230
Career, 8, 22, 31, 55, 56, 59, 67, 79, 87, 112, 235
Carl Jung, 169, 187
child, 31, 32, 33, 34, 35, 36, 37, 39, 40, 41, 42, 43, 44, 45, 46, 48, 49, 50, 51, 52, 53, 78, 99, 100, 170, 182, 194, 206, 215, 217, 220, 224, 228
Childhood, 27, 42, 51, 53, 220
Community, 166, 189

complexity, 16, 17, 19, 37, 66, 72, 87, 89, 103, 107, 155, 160
conformity, 33, 47, 52, 142, 148, 168, 174, 175, 234
conscientious, 14, 56, 71, 115, 231
Conscientiousness, 71
creative, 14, 17, 18, 19, 27, 65, 68, 69, 71, 76, 88, 113, 122, 127, 146, 150, 151, 154, 155, 156, 160, 164, 174, 209, 210, 231, 233, 234
Creativity, 67, 68, 146, 154
Csikszentmihalyi, 9, 72, 74
Curiosity, 140, 144
Dabrowski, 9, 147, 148, 149, 150, 151, 152, 153, 154, 156, 159, 160, 163, 173, 176, 178, 181, 231
Depth of processing, 16, 57
developmental potential, 130, 151, 152, 155, 159, 163, 164, 165
disinhibition, 12, 13, 20, 35, 36, 46, 55, 67, 99, 101, 102, 136, 139, 141, 168, 175, 184
disintegrations, 149
domestic violence, 51

dynamisms, 156, 157, 159
education, 48, 61, 83, 89, 102, 157, 197, 232
Elaine Aron, 5, 22, 23, 220, 225, 228
Emotional Regulation, 172
Emotional responsivity, 17
emotions, 10, 17, 23, 28, 36, 46, 58, 65, 92, 94, 95, 97, 108, 113, 114, 117, 118, 120, 149, 156, 157, 162, 164, 166, 167, 169, 170, 171, 172, 173, 178, 181, 186, 189, 192, 230
empathic, 14, 151, 158, 172, 203
empathy, 10, 17, 21, 36, 37, 57, 60, 61, 62, 71, 91, 114, 115, 142, 156, 167, 174, 180, 181, 190, 232
evolved psychological mechanisms, 4, 5, 20, 173, 190
exercise, 91, 113, 124, 125
Experience and novelty seeking, 40
Experience or novelty seeking, 11
extraverted, 14, 37, 232
Fascinations, 49
Femininity, 181
Five Factor Theory, 8
Flow, 72, 84

Free play, 44, 52
gender, 2, 25, 31, 32, 167, 169, 177, 181, 182, 183, 184, 185, 189
highly sensitive people, 8, 10, 12, 8, 22, 26, 112, 113, 120, 122, 131, 142, 167, 185, 186, 191, 198, 229, 230, 231
human nature, 3
Hydration, 123
impulsive, 46, 47, 48, 82, 104, 137, 138, 168
Intensity, 105, 160
job, 56, 59, 63, 64, 70, 73, 77, 78, 79, 80, 81, 82, 84, 85, 86, 87, 95, 141, 191, 202, 208, 209, 210, 218, 219
late bloomer, 186
looking glass self, 167
love, 6, 38, 39, 51, 55, 63, 77, 80, 90, 91, 92, 93, 94, 95, 99, 104, 107, 108, 109, 122, 131, 136, 141, 161, 162, 183, 204, 206, 216, 226, 229
masculinity, 177, 178, 179, 180, 181, 184, 192
monoamine oxidase, 14, 236
natural selection, 3, 20
Non-Impulsive, 47
openness, 8, 10, 12, 17, 47, 49, 101, 103, 106, 122, 193

Overexcitabilities, 151, 153, 163, 164
Overstimulation, 16, 64, 224
pause and reframe, 118, 172
Personality, 1, 3, 5, 20, 23, 24, 25, 147, 160, 236
personality traits, 12, 1, 2, 3, 5, 6, 8, 10, 21, 25, 39, 41, 55, 78, 178
primary integration, 148, 149
Pushing Through Fear, 101
relationships, 8, 43, 90, 92, 93, 94, 96, 99, 102, 103, 104, 107, 108, 109, 110, 131, 139, 187, 234
resilient, 19, 188
risks, 11, 21, 35, 36, 40, 46, 47, 51, 71, 105, 111, 121, 127, 132, 133, 134, 136, 137, 138, 143, 144, 199, 210, 231, 232
risky behaviors, 133, 139
School, 38
Self-awareness, 108, 114
self-care, 8, 29, 30, 65, 108, 112, 125, 132, 157, 172, 188, 213
Self-employment, 70, 71, 74, 82, 88
Seligman, 9

Sensation seeking, 10, 13, 20, 24, 33, 35, 100, 101, 105, 108, 110, 121, 122, 139, 142, 144, 178, 179, 182, 184, 192, 230, 236
sensory processing sensitivity, 12, 13, 8, 10, 14, 18, 21, 22, 23, 25, 27, 29, 39, 105, 130, 137, 138, 173, 190, 233
Sensory processing sensitivity, 15, 21, 23, 36, 57, 113, 114, 189
Sexuality, 103, 110
Shadow selves, 170
short-term projects, 65, 82, 84, 88, 186
Socialization, 166, 167, 168, 191
spiritual, 76, 112, 125, 126, 127, 128, 129, 131, 132, 159, 175, 188, 191, 197, 225, 226, 227, 234
strategic risk taking, 138
subtleties, 10, 14, 17, 21, 37, 106, 113, 190, 204
Ted Zeff, 22
theory of positive disintegration, 147, 148, 149, 159, 160, 163, 164, 168, 181
thrill and adventure seeking, 11, 13, 14, 20, 35, 40, 44, 47, 55, 67,

231

82, 99, 126, 136, 178, 184
Tracy Cooper, 4, 22, 235
Trade Work, 83
Trait Theory, 1

Trauma, 27
Zuckerman, 5, 10, 11, 24, 46, 47, 49, 102, 133, 139, 236

[1] Hogan, R., Johnson, J., & Briggs, S. (1997). Handbook of personality psychology. Academic Press

[2] Buss, D. (1999) Human nature and individual differences: The evolution of human personality. As cited in Handbook of Personality: Theory and Research, Pervin and John.

[3] Symons, D. (1992). On the use and misuse of Darwinism in the study of human behavior. In J. Barkow, L. Cosmides, & J. Tooby (Eds.). The adapted mind (pp. 137-159). New York: Oxford University Press.

[4] Allport, G., & Odbert, H. (1936). Trait-names: a psycho-lexical study. Psychological Monographs, 47(1), 1-36.

[5] Cattell, R. (1945b). The principal trait clusters for describing personality. Psychological Bulletin, 42, 129-161.

[6] Eysenck, H. (1991). Dimensions of personality: 16, 5, or 3? Criteria for a taxonomy paradigm. Personality and Individual Differences, 12(8), 773–790.

[7] McCrae, R. (1992). The five-factor model: issues and applications. (Special Issue) Journal of Personality, 60.

[8] Zuckerman, M. (1994). Behavioral expressions and biosocial bases of sensation seeking. Cambridge University Press.

[9] Fulker, D., Eysenck, S., & Zuckerman, M. (1980). A genetic and environmental analysis of sensation seeking. Journal of Research in Personality, 14, 261-281.

[10] Zuckerman, M. (2007). Sensation seeking and risky behavior. American Psychological Association. Washington, DC.

[11] Hallman, J., von Korring, a., von Korring., L., & Oreland, L. (1990). Clinical characteristics of female alcoholics with low platelet monoamine oxidase activity. Alcoholism: Clinical and Experimental Research, 14.

[12] Aron, A., & Aron, E. (1997). Sensory-processing sensitivity and its relation to introversion and emotionality. Journal of Personality and

Social Psychology, 73, 345-368.

[13] Aron, A., Aron., E., & Jagiellowicz, J. (2012). Sensory processing sensitivity: A review in the light of the evolution of biological responsivity. Personality and Social Psychology Review, 16, 262-282.

[14] Aron, E. (2010). Psychotherapy and the highly sensitive person: Improving outcomes for that minority of people who are the majority of clients. New York, NY: Routledge.

[15] Jaeger, B. (2004). Making work work for the highly sensitive person. New York, NY: McGraw-Hill.

[16] Bendersky, C., & Shah, N. (2013). The costs of status attainment: Performance effects of individual's status mobility in task groups. Organization Science, 23(2), 308-322.

[17] Munafo, M., Yalcin, B., Willis-Owen, S., & Flint, J. (2008). Association of the dopamine D4 receptor (DRD4) gene and approach-related personality traits: Meta-Analysis and new data. BIOL Psychiatry,63,197-206.

[18] Chen, C., Chen, Chuansheng, Moyzis, R., Stern, H., Qinghua, H., Li, H., Zhu, B., & Dong, Q. (2011). Contributions of dopamine-related genes and environmental factors to highly sensitive personality: A multi-step neuronal system-level approach. PLOS ONE, 6, 1-9.

[19] Cooper, T. (2014). The integral being: A qualitative investigation of highly sensitive persons and temperament-appropriate careers. http://gradworks.umi.com/36/43/3643098.html

[20] Higley, J. D., & Suomi, J. D. (1989). Temperamental reactivity in nonhuman primates. In G. A. Kohnstamm, J. E. Bates, & M. K. Rothbart(Eds.), Temperament in childhood (pp. 152-167). Chichester, England: Wiley.

[21] Nakazawa, D. (2015). Childhood disrupted: How your biography becomes your biology and how you can heal. Simon and Shuster, Inc. New York, NY.

[22] Cooper, T. (2015). Thrive: The highly sensitive person and career. Invictus Publishing, llc. Ozark, MO

[23] Geiwitz, P. (1966). Structure of boredom. Journal of personality

and social psychology, issue 3.

[24] Ryan, R., Deci, E., & Grolnick, W. (1995). Autonomy, relatedness, and the self: Their relation to development and psychopathology. In D. Cicchetti & D. Cohen (Eds.), Developmental Psychopathology (pp. 618–655). New York, NY: Wiley.

[25] Ryan, R., Deci, E., & Grolnick, W. (1995). Autonomy, relatedness, and the self: Their relation to development and psychopathology. In D. Cicchetti & D. Cohen (Eds.), Developmental Psychopathology (pp. 618–655). New York, NY: Wiley.

[26] Aron, E. (1997). The highly sensitive person. Broadway Books.

[27] Csikszentmihalyi, M. (1992a). Flow: The psychology of happiness. London: Harper and Row.

[28] Csikszentmihalyi, M. (2008). Flow: The psychology of optimal experience. HarperCollins. New York, NY.

[29] Lewis, C. (1960). The four loves. New York: Harcourt Brace Jovanovich

[30] Lee, J. (!973). The colors of love: An exploration of the ways of loving. Don Mills, Ontario: New Press.

[31] Lauer, R., & Lauer, J. (2012). Marriage & Family: The quest for intimacy. McGraw Hill, New York: NY.

[32] Mikelson, K., Kessler, R., & Shaver, P. (1997). Adult attachment in a nationally representative sample. Journal of Personality and Social Psychology, 73: 1092-106.

[33] Hartmann, E. (1992). Boundaries in the mind. HarperCollins.

[34] Seligman, M. (2006). Learned optimism: How to change your mind and your life. New York, NY: Random House.

[35] Kjellgren, A., Lindahl, A., & Norlander, T. (2009). Altered states of consciousness and mystical experiences during sensory isolation in flotation tank: Is the highly sensitive personality variable of importance? Imagination, Cognition, and Personality, 29.

[36] Dąbrowski, K. (1975). Foreword. In M. M. Piechowski, A theoretical

and empirical approach to the study of development. Genetic Psychology Monographs, 92, (pp. 233-237).

[37] Piechowski, M. (2008). Discovering Dabrowski's theory. In Mendaglio, S. (Ed.) Dabrowski's theory of positive disintegration, Great Potential Press.
[38] Mika, E. (2008). Dabrowski's views on authentic mental health. In Mendaglio, S. (Ed.) Dabrowski's theory of positive disintegration. Great Potential Press

[39] Dąbrowski, K. (1972). Psychoneurosis is not an illness. London: Gryf Publications.

[40] Dabrowski, K. (1996b). W poszukiwaniu zdrowia psychicznego (In search of mental health). Warszawa: Wydawnictwo Naukowe PWN.

[41] Dąbrowski, K. & Piechowski, M. M. (with Marlene Rankel and Dexter R. Amend). (1996). Multilevelness of emotional and instinctive functions. Part 2: Types and Levels of Development. Lublin, Poland: Towarzystwo Naukowe Katolickiego Uniwersytetu Lubelskiego.

[42] Mendaglio, S. (2008). Dabrowski's theory of positive disintegration: A personality theory for the 21st century. In Mendaglio, S. (Ed.) Dabrowski's theory of positive disintegration, Great Potential Press.

[43] Henslin, J. (2009). Essentials of Sociology. Pearson.

[44] Cooley, C. (1902). Human nature and the social order. New York: Scribners.

[45] Young-Eisendrath, P. and Dawson, T. (1997). The Cambridge Companion to Jung., Cambridge University Press, p. 319

[46] Slater, P. (1970). The pursuit of loneliness. Beacon Press: Boston.

[47] Uhl, J. (2011). Experiences and insights on masculinity by former navy seals in their military and civilian lives. ProQuest.

[48] Robertson, R. (1992). Beginners guide to Jungian psychology. Nicholas-Hays Inc.

37344730R00150

Printed in Poland
by Amazon Fulfillment
Poland Sp. z o.o., Wrocław